Adventures
in Medialand

Behind the News, Beyond the Pundits

Jeff Cohen
and
Norman Solomon

Common Courage Press • Monroe, Maine

Library of Congress Cataloging-in-Publication Data
Cohen, Jeff, 1951-
Adventures in medialand : behind the news, beyond the
pundits
/ Jeff Cohen, Norman Solomon.
p. cm.
ISBN 1-56751-015-9. -- ISBN 1-56751-014-0 (pbk.)
1. Journalism--Political aspects--United States. 2. Press
and politics--United States. 3. United States--Politics
and government--20th century. I. Solomon, Norman.
II. Title.
PN4888.P6C64   1993
071'.3'09045--dc20   93-4092
CIP

Common Courage Press
P.O. Box 702
Monroe, ME 04951
207-525-0900 fax: 207-525-3068

Second Printing

Dedication

To Stephanie and Sequoia

—J.C.

To Cheryl

—N.S.

Contents

Part V
Now It Can Be Told

Part VI
Press and Prejudice

Part VII
Television:
The More You Watch, the Less You Know

Part VIII
Campaign Horse-Racing

Part IX
Robertson, Perot and Other Saviors

Part X
Covering U.S. Power Abroad

Part XI
Fractured History

Part XII
And So It Goes

Introduction

Austin, Texas

Of all the odd misperceptions in the legacy of the Reagan Era (trees cause pollution, people can use food stamps to buy vodka, there's no word for freedom in Russian, etc.) perhaps the oddest is that the news business in this country has a left/liberal bias. As this dubious assumption became an article of faith for millions of Americans, the news business itself demonstrably continued its rightward course.

When Ben Bagdikian first published *The Media Monopoly* in 1982, some 50 corporations controlled most of the major media outlets in the United States: 1,787 daily newspapers; 11,000 magazines; 9,000 radio stations; 1,000 television stations; 2,500 book publishers and seven major movie studios. By the time the fourth edition was released in 1993, the number was down to about 20 corporations, and it is still dropping.

At the end of World War II, 80 percent of American newspapers were independently owned. Today most are controlled by 15 chains. Overall, media owners are conservative. And the trend toward taking political commentators and pundits directly off the frontlines of partisan political warfare, rather than from the ranks of seasoned journalists, has accelerated abruptly: those who served Reagan now writing syndicated columns include Kenneth Adelman, Richard Perle, Mona Charen, Oliver North, Patrick Buchanan, and Jeane Kirkpatrick.

What most people mean when they talk about "the liberal media" is the *New York Times* and the *Washington Post,* neither of which are ever read by 99.25 percent of all Americans. Both *USA Today* and the *Wall Street Journal* have substantially larger circulations. And of course the "leftist bias" of even the supposedly liberal *New York Times* is so dubious that an entire journalism review, *Lies Of Our Times,* and much of the magazine *EXTRA!* are devoted to regularly debunking the supposed bias. Like all other American newspapers, the *Times* and the *Post* are cripplingly dependent on "official sources."

Most Americans who read newspapers, an ever-shrinking coterie, read such epic advocates of boat-rocking as the *Abilene Reporter,* the *Amarillo Globe,* the *Dallas Morning News,* the *Lubbock Avalanche-Journal,* the *Houston Chronicle,* the *San Antonio Express,* the *El Paso Times,* etc. Just try a quick survey of the newspapers in your home state and see how liberal you think they are.

In refreshing counterpoint to this onslaught of vapid status quo-ism stands FAIR, Fairness & Accuracy In Reporting, which has a dicey mission. It would help no one if FAIR were simply the liberal equivalent of AIM (Accuracy In Media), the right-wing outfit that claims to be a media watchdog organization. Anyone who has dealt with AIM and its founder, Reed Irvine, as I did while serving on the National News Council, quickly finds that AIM's purpose is not to encourage accuracy but to engage in tendentious right-wing political argument. While it would be nice to think that there was someone out there on the other end of the seesaw jumping up and down like mad to bring the media into some kind of balance, in fact, the very concept of balance is one of the central problems of the American press.

The very notion that on any given story all you have to do is report what both sides say and you've done a fine job of objective journalism debilitates the press. There is no such thing as objectivity, and the truth, that slippery little bugger, has the oddest habit of being way to hell off on one side or the other: it seldom nestles neatly halfway between any two opposing points of view. The smug complacency of much of the press—I have heard many an editor say, "Well, we're being attacked by both sides, so we must be right"— stems from the curious notion that if you get a quote from someone on both sides, preferably in an official position, you've done the job. In the first place, most stories aren't two-sided, they're 17-sided at least. In the second place, it's of no help to either the readers or the truth to quote one side saying, "Cat," and the other side saying "Dog," while the truth is there's an elephant crashing around out there in the bushes. Getting up off your duff and going to find out for yourself is still the most useful thing a reporter can do.

I believe the press's most serious failures are not its sins of commission, but its sins of omission—the stories we miss, the stories we don't see, the stories that don't hold press conferences, the stories that don't come from "reliable sources."

Jeff Cohen and Norman Solomon have attacked all this and more with energy, brio and the occasional display of a mordant sense of humor. It's grand to see their work, normally scattered in publications of modest circulation, collected so we can relish it at one swell foop, as one of my favorite Texas politicians used to say. Cohen and Solomon, both associated with FAIR, have solved the problem of "whose side are you on?" by being on the side of the reader, the viewer, the Joe or the Annie out there making an honest living fixing cars or grooming poodles while trying to make sense of the public debate in their spare time.

So dive in and enjoy some of the best press-bashing, honest sleuthing, news-consumer tips and happy hell-raising with the powers-that-be to be found anywhere. Way to go, guys. More, more!

Molly Ivins

Part I
The Media Elite

"The most sacred cow of the press is the press itself," the great independent journalist George Seldes observed long ago. Today giant media institutions pose as guardians of the public interest. But don't expect those news outlets to be very candid about who's running the media show.

Can the Press Cover
the Old Boys Club
That Owns It?

It was pure luck that a Time Warner journalist ran into a Time Warner executive at a redwood retreat 70 miles north of San Francisco. It was also bad luck, at least for the journalist. The Time Warner executive threw him out.

You see, it wasn't just any retreat. The chance meeting occurred at the exclusive, super-secret Bohemian Grove where the old boys of America's government and corporate elite gather each summer for two weeks of laid-back schmoozing and speechmaking, not to mention the club's mock-Druid fire rituals.

And it wasn't just any journalist. Dirk Mathison was, until recently, the enterprising San Francisco bureau chief of *People* magazine, owned by Time Warner. An uninvited guest (reporters are banned from Bohemian Grove), Mathison hiked over back-country trails to sneak into the Grove's July 1991 "encampment" three different times. The third time was no charm for Mathison: that's when he ran into the Time Warner executive who recognized him and tossed him out.

Mathison had already learned a lot. Contrary to the claims of the Grove, Mathison saw that the male-only retreat is not just innocent summertime relaxation. Newsworthy events occur there. Former Secretary of the Navy John Lehman, for example, gave a lecture in which he stated that the Pentagon estimated 200,000 Iraqis were killed during the six weeks of the Gulf War. The Pentagon believes the public is not ready to hear the death count; among friends, Lehman felt no need to go dumb on the subject. The title of his speech: "Smart Weapons."

Other speakers included Defense Secretary Richard

Cheney and former Health, Education and Welfare Secretary Joseph Califano, speaking on "America's Health Revolution—Who Lives, Who Dies, Who Pays." Former Attorney General Elliot Richardson titled his speech "Defining the New World Order." That definition is sought by millions of Americans, but the speech wasn't aired on C-SPAN.

Expecting to read all about it in *People*? Don't count on it. Even though Mathison embarked on the Bohemian Grove story with his editors' approval, and even though Mathison says his article was so well received that extra space was alloted for it, the story was mysteriously killed.

People's managing editor told our researchers that while he had authorized Mathison to infiltrate the Grove, he later killed the piece (denying any input from Time Warner higher-ups) after realizing that he had authorized "trespassing."

Mathison believes the reason *People* editors spiked the story "had to do with their bosses, not mine." He warned us we might never pin down the full explanation: "It's easier to penetrate the Bohemian Grove than the Time-Life Building."

One need not penetrate the Time-Life Building to realize what this episode says about journalism today. It tells us how difficult it can be for journalists to report fully on America's political and economic elite when their bosses are loyal members of that elite.

Every year at Bohemian Grove, media executives hobnob with newsmakers. Walter Cronkite, for example, resides at the same lodge at the Grove as George Bush. But media figures enter into a pact of silence, agreeing that the Grove—whose membership has included every Republican president since Coolidge, and on whose premises presidential campaigns were fueled and the Manhattan (A-bomb) Project conceived—is off-limits to news coverage.

Since the Grove is such a closed institution, it is admittedly difficult for journalists to cover. But what about related issues that are out in the open, and should be easier to cover? For example, how tough can we expect major media to be in reporting on corporate mergers and executive greed in an era of middle-class downturn and layoffs?

Well, working journalists are part of that middle class, with reason to be cautious. After Time merged with Warner to form the biggest media firm in the world, Time Warner chair Steve Ross told *Variety* that journalists "cannot afford to be anywhere but part of a strong, diverse company with global reach and responsibility... A diverse, financially strong media company makes it possible for managers to attract and nurture talented journalists."

Instead of nurturing journalists, Time Warner—thanks largely to debt incurred during the merger—recently laid off 600 magazine employees, including 19 of *Time*'s 75 correspondents.

What makes the layoffs doubly bitter is that Time Warner's Steve Ross—thanks largely to the merger—was the country's highest compensated chief executive in 1990, "earning" $78 million in salary and stock. That's enough money to have retained all the laid-off employees, with $48 million to spare.

Ironically, the analyst who compiled the list of highest paid executives for *Fortune,* a Time Warner-owned publication, announced in June 1991 he could no longer work there. His reason: interference from Time Warner management, especially when it came to estimating the compensation of Steve Ross.

And what about Dirk Mathison, the enterprising journalist who tried to cover the lords of free enterprise? He was one of the 600 laid off by Time Warner.

November 26, 1991

The Real Media Elite

Dan Quayle is on the warpath, denouncing a "media elite" which has nothing but "scorn" for people who uphold "basic moral values." From newsrooms and sitcom studios, says Quayle, this elite looks down on "average Americans."

When Dan Quayle attacks the "media elite," it's like Arnold Schwarzenegger decrying the evils of body-building.

Quayle is much closer to the media elite than he lets on. His family owns a chain of newspapers, including the most powerful papers in Indiana and Arizona. He personally owns $400,000 worth of stock in Central Newspapers Inc.

Vice President Quayle would have you believe that the media elite is biased against conservative politicians like him. But this claim doesn't square with the fact that of the daily newspapers making presidential endorsements in 1988, about 70 percent backed the Bush-Quayle ticket.

Far from being the liberal chorus that Quayle describes, the media's loudest voices are conservative—some so far right they think Quayle is too liberal.

On radio, for example, no one has more opinion-shaping power than extreme conservative Rush Limbaugh. On national TV, only two political pundits—both conservative—have become ubiquitous enough to appear every day of the week: John McLaughlin and Patrick Buchanan. Among the most widely published political columnists, four of the top seven write from the right: George Will, James Kilpatrick, William Safire and William F. Buckley Jr.

There is a media elite in this country. But that elite is corporate establishment. After a decade of mergers, takeovers and newspaper closings, media power has concentrated into fewer—and more conservative—hands. Look at the managers of companies such as Time Warner, General

Electric, Dow Jones, Cap Cities/ABC, and you'll have a good idea who is in the media elite.

Also, take a look at the media's biggest advertisers—General Motors, Philip Morris, Procter & Gamble, DuPont, etc.—companies with the power to muzzle viewpoints that offend them.

Imagine, for example, that Rush Limbaugh had a change of heart one day about how to use his pulpit of 500 radio stations. Imagine that instead of scapegoating "environmental extremists," gays and "feminazis" as the forces ruining our country, he began attacking by name the "greedy corporations" that "pollute the earth, rip off consumers and export good American jobs to slave laborers in the Third World." How many weeks would it take before his sponsors pulled the plug?

When Dan Quayle castigates the media elite, he certainly does not mean the media owners or sponsors (most of whom are Republicans) or the political pundits (most of whom are fairly conservative).

Like the "media criticism" of Vice President Spiro Agnew more than two decades ago, Quayle has political goals in mind: intimidating media professionals into softer coverage of the White House, and corralling the votes of social and religious conservatives who are offended by the media.

Quayle's speeches echo Agnew's. In 1969, Agnew denounced "liberal" media snobs who "do not represent the views of America." Lately, Vice President Quayle has denounced the media in these words: "It sometimes seems we have two cultures—the cultural elite, and the rest of us... They're embarrassed about the views of the average American—because moral values are what the American people care most about."

There *is* a serious critique to be made of the media elite and its moral values. This elite values one thing above all else—maximizing profit. Worship of the "bottom line" seems to take precedence over family, community and country.

That's why the TV industry insists on bombarding our kids with ads for candy and sugar-coated cereal every Saturday morning; why so many magazines advertise cigarettes while avoiding tough coverage of the tobacco industry; why TV ratings periods are endless parades of sexual titillation; and why TV stations serve up such edifying programs as "Studs," "Geraldo" and "Gorgeous Ladies of Wrestling."

Dan Quayle can't seriously address the elite's moral bankruptcy because he is ideologically committed to the one value these media corporations revere: profiteering. Of course Quayle—and the media managers—have a prettier-sounding name for it. They call it "free enterprise."

[Epilogue: Three months after leaving the vice-presidency, Dan Quayle joined the board of Central Newspapers Inc.]

June 17, 1992

The *Washington Post*:
Too Close to Power

When the owner of the *Washington Post* threw a dinner party for Bill Clinton and Al Gore a few weeks after their electoral victory, she raised her glass in a toast. "These occasions have value," Katharine Graham said candidly. "They create relationships beyond the office."

The mood was similar when the Democratic Party's key financial backer, Pamela Harriman, hosted a private celebration for the Clinton-Gore duo. Graham and other top executives of the *Post* were among the elite guests.

Swaddled in legend since Watergate two decades ago, the *Washington Post* retains an anti-establishment image that is among the most absurd myths in journalism today. Together with the *New York Times* (whose conservative columnist William Safire wrote approvingly of the Graham dinner), the *Post* largely sets the national media agenda.

The *Post* carries enormous weight within the U.S. government...and vice versa. Officials often float their trial balloons and selective leaks via the *Post*, which routinely draws its hot stories from unnamed sources in high places.

The newspaper's ownership has long been entwined with powerful—and sometimes shadowy—government figures. Several decades ago, Katharine Graham's husband Philip was close friends with CIA spymasters Allen Dulles, Richard Helms, Frank Wisner and Desmond FitzGerald, as well as with John F. Kennedy.

A memo from Philip Graham urged JFK to choose Lyndon Johnson as his running mate in 1960. Graham, the *Post*'s publisher, knew ahead of time about many covert operations, including the shameful 1961 Bay of Pigs invasion of Cuba; the advance knowledge was not shared with *Post* readers.

After Graham's suicide in 1963, his widow carried on

the tradition of social intimacy with Washington's power elite—and willingness to maintain secrecy. "There have been instances," Katharine Graham acknowledges, "in which secrets have been leaked to us which we thought were so dangerous that we went to them [U.S. officials] and told them that they had been leaked to us and did not print them."

In a speech to senior CIA officials at the agency's headquarters in November 1988, Katharine Graham defended such self-censorship. "There are some things the general public does not need to know and shouldn't," she said. "I believe democracy flourishes when the government can take legitimate steps to keep its secrets and when the press can decide whether to print what it knows."

But what about the *Post*'s reputation for aggressive journalism, earned in the early 1970s? It's true that in June 1971, a year before it began breaking Watergate stories, the *Post* jumped into the breach when a court enjoined the *New York Times* from continuing to publish the Pentagon Papers. Katharine Graham gave the go-ahead for the *Post* to print the top-secret documents detailing U.S. mendacities during the Vietnam War.

In previous years, however, those falsehoods had been greatly aided by the *Washington Post*. In 1968, President Johnson was so grateful for pro-war editorials written by *Post* editor Russell Wiggins that he appointed Wiggins to be U.S. ambassador to the United Nations.

Some of the main architects of the Vietnam War were close friends of Katharine Graham, including Defense Secretary Robert McNamara, who later joined the board of directors of the Washington Post Company. (The current board includes the past or present heads of Johnson & Johnson, Coca-Cola and H.J. Heinz.)

After the *Post*'s Watergate coverage helped drive Richard Nixon from the White House, there were concerns that the paper was overstepping. Executive editor Ben Bradlee later conceded to author Mark Hertsgaard: "The criticism was that we were going on too much, and trying to make a Watergate out of everything. And I think we were sensitive to that criticism much more than we should have been, and that we did ease off."

The next Republican to be elected president benefitted a great deal as the *Post* "eased off." The newspaper boosted many of Ronald Reagan's policies. It didn't hurt that his wife Nancy and Katharine Graham became good friends.

Some *Post* staffers have privately wondered whether the newspaper would have been as aggressive in reporting on Watergate if key figures in the Nixon Administration had established such personal ties with Mrs. Graham.

When the Iran-Contra scandal was getting her down, Nancy Reagan received solace from Graham and the *Post*'s editorial page editor Meg Greenfield, who expressed their sympathies during many lunches and phone conversations.

Closely intertwined with the highest echelons of government by social relations, shared attitudes and corporate connections, the *Post* has been part of a widespread journalistic failure. The *Post* ignored or downplayed major stories like Iran-Contra and Savings & Loans until government officials got around to providing leaks, pronouncements or indictments.

The sad truth is that scoops in the *Washington Post* are often a consequence of the newspaper's close ties with government powers-that-be. Those are the kind of "relationships" that Katharine Graham was toasting at her party for Bill Clinton and Al Gore.

December 30, 1992

Part II
The Pundits

They never seem to stop pontificating about the issues of the day. Accountable only to the institutions that pay them, the nation's masters of punditry hold forth on the TV networks and in widely-syndicated columns. They run a narrow gamut...endlessly...setting the bounds of political non-debate.

"IN THE NEXT HALF HOUR, MY WEALTHY WHITE CONSERVATIVE MALE FRIENDS AND I WILL DISCUSS THE ANNOYINGLY PERSISTENT BLACK UNDER-CLASS, AND WHY WOMEN GET SO EMOTIONAL ABOUT ABORTION."

Term Limits
For Political Pundits

Now for a truly grassroots initiative: term limits for political pundits.

They're powerful. They're entrenched. And they serve us no better than the politicians do.

We're talking about the Washington pundits who dominate network TV. Some have been "inside the Beltway" longer than the men who chair key congressional committees…and that's saying something.

The "hot-air brigade" can fill hour after hour of broadcasts with political trivia—polls, personalities, peccadillos, predictions—while rarely offending any powerful interests. They're far too cozy with the Washington elite they cover.

With mainstream pundits focused on various distractions, crucial issues are rarely discussed. For example, look at what passed for "post-election analysis" when it turned out—after all the hype about career politicians running scared—that 1992 was *the year of the incumbent,* as usual.

Pundits and others in the national media seemed almost clueless to explain the triumph of U.S. Senate and House incumbents. The best the *New York Times* could do was to report that Senate incumbents "somehow managed to survive."

There was an obvious—and unstated—answer to the puzzle: M-O-N-E-Y. Many of these incumbents raised two or three times as much money for their campaigns as the challengers they narrowly defeated. This was the case for senators like Alfonse D'Amato (New York), Arlen Specter (Pennsylvania) and Bob Packwood (Oregon).

In a column six months ago, we challenged national media to report which candidates won more "votes per dollar spent." Reporting this VPDS count would make it clear that many incumbents would have been defeated if not for their advantage in dollars.

But most televised pundits don't follow the money. The big-bucks special interests dominating Washington are almost a taboo subject.

It shouldn't be so difficult to point out that—while the Bush family is moving out and the Clinton family is moving in—the corporate money that greatly influences both major parties isn't moving anywhere. It's part of the "permanent government."

In recent months, Arco has been lobbying to be able to drill for oil in Alaska's Arctic Wildlife Refuge. Not coincidentally, Arco has been "double giving"—donating heavily to both parties, nearly $1 million in the last two years. Clinton's campaign chair, Mickey Kantor, is a partner in a law firm that lobbies for Arco. These facts are known to mainstream pundits but are rarely reported.

Or take the case of Dwayne Andreas, chair of the Archer Daniels Midland (ADM) grain company that produces 70 percent of the nation's ethanol. A PBS "Frontline" documentary revealed that after Andreas donated $400,000 to the Republican Party, his company received a Clean Air Act waiver for ethanol.

Think Andreas' role in Washington is played down by the big pundits because they just don't know about it? Think again.

Andreas and his company not only fund the Republicans, they also pay some of the pundits' salaries. ADM is a longstanding sponsor of political pundit shows from John McLaughlin on PBS to ABC's "This Week With David Brinkley," NBC's "Meet the Press" and CBS's "Face the Nation." Brinkley, leaders of both parties and Andreas own vacation condos in the same Florida beach building.

No one is alleging a conspiracy here in which establishment pundits consciously censor the real news while diverting public attention to political trivia. The problem is that these pundits are so immersed in the system—so close to the political and corporate interests controlling it—that they don't question it.

Since they accept big-money dominance of politics (and TV) as a given, mass media's pundits don't consider political news to encompass the day-to-day workings of power and influence. Instead, what's "newsworthy" are the techniques of campaigning, or dramatic battles on Capitol Hill.

And when these pundits speak out against the influence of "special interests" in politics, they usually focus on blacks, women, labor, seniors and similar groups—not the big-money guys.

Like the career politicians they cover, many long-time pundits have been corrupted by the system and don't even seem to know it.

The 1992 election produced a slightly more diverse Congress—more women, more racial minorities, more citizen activists.

But there are no elections for the pundit elite. Maybe term limitation is the answer.

While we're at it, financial disclosure is also needed: When TV pundits discuss issues affecting the finances of their sponsors—whether ADM or whoever—viewers should be told.

November 11, 1992

HEY, CITIZENS--CONFUSED ABOUT THE *ISSUES*? MAYBE YOU SHOULD SPEND MORE TIME WATCHING THE ENDLESS PARADE OF *COMMENTATORS* AND *EXPERTS* ON THE *TV NEWS*!

BLAH!

BLAH!

BLAH! BLAH!

THEY HAVE *THREE PIECE SUITS* AND *IMPRESSIVE-SOUNDING CREDENTIALS*!

--JOINING US NOW FROM THE RESEARCH INSTITUTE FOR CULTURAL ANALYSIS OF POLICY STUDIES--

THEY REPRESENT THE *WIDE SPECTRUM* OF MAINSTREAM POLITICAL DISCOURSE--

--FROM THE *MIDDLE OF THE ROAD*--

--TO THE *EXTREME RIGHT WING*!

WE DON'T KNOW ABOUT *YOU*, BUT *WE'RE* SURE GRATEFUL THAT THESE DISPASSIONATE ANALYSTS ARE WILLING TO SHARE THEIR KEEN, UNBIASED INSIGHTS WITH *US*!

--STATISTICS *CLEARLY* PROVE THAT THE NIXON ADMINISTRATION'S FOREIGN POLICY WAS THE *FINEST* THIS COUNTRY HAS EVER SEEN!

Great Moments
in Pundit History

Too often we forget to pause and give credit to the pundits who hand down so much wisdom to the rest of us.

The chosen few are usually white guys—though they've recently allowed a few women and blacks into the club...as long as they sound just like the other club members.

If we could harness the wind this group generates on the airwaves and in print, it might solve our nation's energy problems.

Here, then, are a few of the shining moments brought to us by the country's most highly touted political pundits:

Election Wisdom

- In October 1980, columnist George Will went on ABC "Nightline" to praise Ronald Reagan's "thoroughbred performance" in a crucial debate with incumbent President Jimmy Carter. But there was something Will didn't tell us viewers: He had helped coach Reagan for that debate—and had read Carter briefing materials stolen from the White House.

- In 1987, acclaimed political analyst David Broder wrote columns about how George Bush was "too innocent" and "too nice" to enter into a tough campaign for president. The next year, Willie Horton ads and ACLU-bashing propelled Bush into the Oval Office.

- Beginning in 1989, pundits hailed centrist Virginia Governor Douglas Wilder as the great black hope who could push Jesse Jackson to the margins. The *Washington Post*'s Juan Williams praised Wilder as a "rebuke" to Jackson, calling the governor "arguably the most important black American politician of the 20th century." Boosted by such puffery, Wilder entered the '92 presidential race; he failed to survive the first primary. Four years earlier, Jackson had won 7 million Democratic votes, about 30 percent of all ballots cast.

Public Health

● In a 1979 *Newsweek* column, George Will denounced the movie "The China Syndrome"—which dramatized a nuclear reactor accident—as hysterical Hollywood propaganda. "Nuclear plants," Will scoffed, "like color-TV sets, give off minute amounts of radiation, but there is more cancer risk in sitting next to a smoker than next to a nuclear plant." Will's column was still on newsstands when the real-life Three Mile Island nuclear nightmare began.

● In 1986, William F. Buckley proclaimed in a *New York Times* column: "Everyone detected with AIDS should be tattooed in the upper forearm, to protect common-needle users, and on the buttocks, to prevent the victimization of other homosexuals." Under fire for a plan reminiscent of Nazi Germany, Buckley later withdrew the suggestion because "it proved socially intolerable."

Racial Awareness

● "I know something of racists," columnist James J. Kilpatrick wrote dramatically in 1989. "I was one." After the 1954 Supreme Court decision barring segregation in public schools, "To my regret it took the better part of 10 years for me to realize that racial discrimination is wrong, wrong, wrong." Admirable self-criticism? Not quite. Kilpatrick's admission was the preamble to a column decrying modern-day civil rights marchers who "have only an abstract, theoretical interest in a color-blind Constitution."

● On PBS's "MacNeil/Lehrer NewsHour" in 1990, pundit Mark Shields argued that—unlike Ronald Reagan—George Bush was supportive of the interests of black people and civil rights. On National Public Radio the previous year, Cokie Roberts referred matter-of-factly to "George Bush's pro-civil rights record." Neither Shields nor Roberts mentioned that Bush had opposed the landmark 1964 Civil Rights Act. Not long after the two pundits had certified his civil rights credentials, Bush began assailing key new civil rights legislation as a "quota bill."

Humility

● Some pundits are so brilliant they don't need to analyze something in order to render a judgment. On ABC's "This Week With David Brinkley," Cokie Roberts denounced the movie "JFK"—sight unseen: "My father was a member of the Warren Commission... I will not see the movie. I do not see any point in going to see and paying money to a person who is discrediting a lot of very good men."

● Perhaps these pundits are off the mark so often because they're too close to an establishment that's frequently disinforming them, and us. In a moment of candor, ABC's Sam Donaldson acknowledged: "I practice what most people in my profession practice... As a rule, we are, if not handmaidens of the establishment, at least blood brothers to the establishment... We end up the day usually having some version of what the White House has suggested as a story."

The next time you hear someone praising the pundits who soak up so much air time and so much ink, you might mention that wisdom is in the eye of the beholder. If we don't think for ourselves, there are plenty of media "experts" ready to do it for us.

June 3, 1992

TV's Political Spectrum: The Best That Money Can Buy

Turn on TV's political talk shows, and you'll witness a clamorous debate over President Clinton's economic plan. The discussion is often so heated that it looks like a free-for-all offering every imaginable viewpoint.

Look again.

Some perspectives are very loud. Others are barely audible.

Certain commentators laud Clinton for a "bold and courageous plan" that "spreads the pain evenly" and will "recharge the economy and reduce the deficit."

Other commentators denounce the Clinton plan as "tax and spend liberalism" that "encourages class conflict" and—according to conservative pundit Robert Novak—"socialism."

But if TV is your main source of news and views, you may not know that there is a third point-of-view: Some analysts criticize the plan because it taxes corporations and the wealthy too timidly and middle-income people too harshly, while failing to seriously cut the bloated military budget.

Proponents of this third view emphasize that the richest 1 percent of Americans (average yearly income $567,000) saved more than $71 billion last year—a big chunk of the budget deficit—from federal tax breaks enacted since 1978.

This perspective—suggesting bigger tax hikes on wealthy individuals whose incomes boomed in the last decade—might well be popular with the public. Unfortunately, TV viewers almost never hear it.

That's because political shows on television are shaped by a subtle—and pervasive—form of economic censorship.

The same business interests that spread campaign

contributions around Washington to narrow policy debates (see William Greider's book *Who Will Tell The People*) use their ownership and sponsorship of TV to narrow media debates (see Ben Bagdikian's *The Media Monopoly*).

Rather than a full political spectrum, the mass media spectrum often extends from GE to GM.

Take CNN's "Capital Gang," a boisterous Beltway show that features four regular panelists who rarely take positions that would offend program sponsor General Electric. Rightists Robert Novak and Mona Charen debate what passes for "leftists" on American television—Al Hunt, Washington bureau chief of the *Wall Street Journal*, and columnist Mark Shields, whose literature boasts that he "is free of any political tilt."

When the *Wall Street Journal* represents the left, the spectrum is hardly full. It extends from the center to the right.

On "Capital Gang," Novak and Charen predictably savaged Clinton's economic plan, while Hunt and Shields defended it with minor reservations. Hunt apparently would prefer more cuts in seniors' benefits.

As usual on network TV politics shows, all criticism came from the right, and none from the left.

Given the parameters of the debate, no wonder "Capital Gang" guest George Stephanopoulos, Clinton's spokesperson, felt the need to defend his boss by saying he's "got a pro-business slant" in the budget plan.

Throughout the 1980s, conservative commentators gained increasing dominance on TV. The weekly PBS program hosted by Bill Buckley, founder of the right-wing *National Review* magazine, persevered thanks to funding from corporations and conservative foundations.

Columnist George Will, who'd been a Washington editor of the *National Review*, became ABC-TV's lone commentator—later matched up with ABC correspondent Sam Donaldson, whose voice is loud but hardly left.

John McLaughlin, another Washington editor of *Na-*

tional Review, emerged from relative obscurity in the early 1980s to become one of the first political pundits appearing on national TV every day of the week—as host of three different programs. It all started with the center-right "Mc-Laughlin Group," underwritten for "public" television by GE at a cost of over $1 million per year.

While McLaughlin might have you believe his prominence on TV stems from his superior knowledge and good looks, he and his colleagues owe their prominence to having the viewpoints big corporations are willing to sponsor.

GE, Pepsico, Archer Daniels Midland and the half-dozen other firms that heavily sponsor TV politics programs are not about to bankroll three national shows per week hosted by consumer advocate Ralph Nader, or populist Jim Hightower, or democratic socialist Barbara Ehrenreich. It's this hidden economic hand that imparts the slant to TV discourse.

The problem with television's political spectrum is not the abundance of conservatives, but the absence of unapologetic progressives. Editors and alumni of the *National Review* are household names; how many TV watchers can identify a single editor from a left magazine like *The Nation?*

Al Hunt, Mark Shields, Michael Kinsley, Jack Germond and Eleanor Clift are not advocates for progressive causes. They are more or less centrists. Their motto seems to be: "I'm not a leftist, but I play one on TV."

If you have watched PBS's "MacNeil/Lehrer News-Hour," sponsored over the years by AT&T and Pepsico, you've seen a pundit pairing of Shields and David Gergen that stays safely within establishment bounds.

Though many regular TV commentators advocate conservative and pro-corporate policies, virtually no one on network television advocates such measures as tax-financed national health insurance, or federally sponsored day-care, or government programs to ensure that everyone who wants a job has a job.

Extreme or fringe ideas? According to *New York Times*

polls, these rarely-discussed proposals are favored by majorities of the public.

Imagine how popular these proposals would be if articulate advocates were allowed to promote them day after day on CNN, PBS and the other TV networks.

February 24, 1993

TV's Political Spectrum

Pat Buchanan, Fred Barnes,
John McLaughlin, David Gergen,
Robert Novak, William F. Buckley, George Will

Sam Donaldson, Mark Shields, Michael Kinsley,
Morton Kondrake, Al Hunt,
Jack Germond, Hodding Carter

Part III
Be True to Your Class: Corporate Spin

Describing the mission of his St. Louis Post-Dispatch *in 1907, publisher Joseph Pulitzer wrote that it would "always oppose privileged classes and public plunderers, and never lack sympathy with the poor." Few mainstream media outlets utter such principles today. Instead, they boast of fairly covering all sectors of the public. In reality, certain classes get better coverage than others.*

"Geezer-Bashing"
And Other Budget Bias

Bill Clinton's 1993 economic package deserves credit for spurring at least one growth industry—the instant rise in media reporting and commentary on the U.S. budget.

The boom in media analysis of the Clinton plan sparked some incisive reporting, but much of the coverage simply highlighted longstanding biases and blind-spots of the national press corps.

"Geezer-Bashing"

The consensus among mainstream reporters and pundits is that courageous politicians must "stand up to" the seniors—often portrayed as greedy or spoiled, and unwilling to sacrifice.

As President Clinton prepared his economic plan, for example, NBC's John Chancellor offered this February 1993 commentary: "Governing means deciding who gets what and when they get it. One group did really well from 1980 to 1990: Households headed by people over 65…. If you made a movie about who gets what, you could call it: 'Honey, We Robbed the Kids.'"

Chancellor's analysis of 1980s robbers neatly overlooked S&L looters, junk bond dealers, corporate takeover artists, and his boss General Electric—owner of NBC—which helped write the 1981 corporate tax law that slashed its own taxes to below zero.

Clinton's plan would raise taxes on Social Security benefits of couples with combined incomes above $32,000 and individuals above $25,000. Such seniors were referred to by reporters as "well-to-do." Sixteen thousand dollars each for grandma and for grandpa hardly makes them "well-to-do."

Given media vitriol aimed at "greedy" seniors, much

of the public may not realize that Social Security benefits are the main sustenance of most elderly Americans, and are all that keeps a third of them above the poverty line.

Advocates for seniors—far less visible in the media than "geezer-bashers"—warn that "means testing" of Social Security recipients would transform this popular insurance system into a welfare program vulnerable to further cuts. Rather than monkey with Social Security to exclude well-off seniors, these advocates call for increasing taxes on all wealthy Americans—young, middle-aged or elderly.

Overlooking Pentagon Largess

News reports referred to "deep defense cuts" in Clinton's economic plan. Many Americans might be surprised to learn that Clinton's first-year budget sought only a 4 percent reduction from George Bush's proposed military funding—mostly through trimming personnel and a salary freeze.

Costly weapons systems, many developed to fight a Soviet Union that no longer exists, remain in the budget virtually untouched. Treasury Secretary Lloyd Bentsen—aptly called "Loophole Lloyd" by the *Village Voice*'s Doug Ireland—is credited with saving the V-22 Osprey aircraft (which Bush's Defense Department tried to cancel) and other expensive projects important to Texas. It was reported in *Defense News*, but not in big media, that Defense Secretary Les Aspin actually rejected budget cuts proposed by the Army and Air Force.

Day after day TV pundits beseech politicians to "take on entitlements and Social Security" to reduce the deficit. Rarely does anyone on TV demand deficit-reducing cuts in the post-Cold War military.

When national media do report on military cutbacks, the issue of job loss is paramount, as it should be. But during the 12 years that Republicans cut other federal programs—housing, for example—job loss was little more than a footnote in news coverage.

Soothe-the-Rich

While polls show that raising taxes on corporations and the wealthy is overwhelmingly popular, that's not the case among powerful pundits—who attack Clinton's small, loophole-ridden tax increases on the wealthy as "soak the rich" tactics. After the 1992 election, ABC's David Brinkley told a trucking industry group that raising taxes on the well-to-do was a "sick, stupid joke" and "cheap demagoguery."

Even full implementation of Clinton's income tax hikes on rich Americans would still leave them among the lowest-taxed in the advanced industrial countries. But the whining by the megapundits does make certain selfish sense. They're in the top income-brackets themselves: George Will's income is a reported $1.5 million yearly; Patrick Buchanan made over $800,000 in 1991, according to election filings; the Evans and Novak team grosses an estimated $1 million per year, as does John McLaughlin.

Decrying "Class War"

A *Washington Post* news article (headlined "Is Clinton Pitting Class Against Class?") spoke of Clinton's "soak the rich" desires and his "populist provisions"—such as a curb on corporate deductions for country club dues. During the 1980s, when changes in the tax code abetted one of the most dramatic transfers of wealth from one class to another—that is, from working-class Americans to the rich—it was hard to find a news story headlined: "Is Reagan Pitting Class Against Class?"

Neglecting the Poor

On March 16, 1964, President Lyndon Johnson declared a "national war on poverty" that would be waged until "total victory." Nearly 30 years later, few in the media question Clinton's tacit acceptance of poverty. While mass media are quick to declare various crises—drugs, terrorism, the shortage of single men—they are generally blasé about the crisis of poverty. One out of five children, and one out of two black children, live below the *official* poverty line—a line rigged by the federal government to undercount the poor.

National media should do some re-budgeting of their own: Trim away biases that support wealthy interests, and increase expenditures to cover the economic interests of poor and middle-income Americans.

March 3, 1993

Specter of Class Warfare Haunts Media

When Karl Marx predicted 150 years ago that Europe would witness a bitter struggle between workers and owners, even he couldn't imagine that his scenario of class warfare "would play in Peoria." But for months in 1992 it did play in Peoria, Illinois, the conservative, middle-American city where unionized and skilled factory workers battled the powerful Caterpillar manufacturing company.

The Peoria strike is over for now, but rest assured that national media will continue to be haunted by the specter of class warfare. They find it even where it doesn't exist— places like Capitol Hill and the presidential campaign trail.

Of course the American people dislike anything that smacks of class warfare. How do we know? News media tell us so.

Representative Richard Gephardt is about as Marxist as Donald Trump. But in 1989 when Gephardt launched a brief crusade against White House efforts to reduce the capital gains tax, you would have thought he'd recited the *Communist Manifesto* from memory and inserted it into the Congressional Record.

A *Washington Post* news story faulted Gephardt and other Democrats in Congress for using "class-warfare rhetoric." Two days later a news article in the *Christian Science Monitor* concluded, "The lesson is this: In a nation of people with ambitions to be affluent themselves, someday, class warfare does not sell."

Throughout his presidential campaign Paul Tsongas embraced this "lesson"—calling for a halt to "class warfare," which he charged with harming the nation's industrial base. Recommending capital gains tax cuts, Tsongas urged that attention "not be focused on a myopic discourse about who benefits the most under such a system." In other words, when the rich keep getting richer, they'll have more crumbs dropping from their table for the rest of us. (Crumble-down economics.)

During his stint as media darling, Tsongas presented himself as a political Marcus Welby, M.D., offering bitter pills for the ailing economy. Yet his economic prescriptions were laced with dubious medicines, such as the notion that "American companies should be released from anti-trust constraints in areas which impact on their capabilities in international trade."

By and large, mass media have endorsed the Tsongas approach. In sharp contrast, Jerry Brown's denunciations of wealthy privilege didn't go over well with mainstream media.

The media judgment on Brown is that he used to practice the same big-money politics he now runs against. If you denounce the wealthy contributors you once depended on, this is seen as hypocrisy; if you still depend on them, this is seen as "electability."

The class bias of national media is also apparent in the way tax issues have been covered in recent years. Media jargon is typically topsy-turvy. During the 1980s, proposals for tax breaks to the wealthy were regularly termed "tax reform." Reaganomics enriched the already-rich at the expense of most other Americans, but news accounts never called it "class warfare" on behalf of the well-to-do.

When the Reagan Administration slashed the tax rate on the wealthiest Americans from 70 to around 30 percent, that was labeled "conservative." In 1988, when Jesse Jackson proposed raising the rate to 38.5 percent, that was called "radical" and "far left."

At the 1988 Democratic Convention, Jackson pushed for a tax freeze on the middle class and poor, and a tax hike only for wealthy individuals and corporations. Reporters routinely described it simply as a plan "for higher taxes."

When the Jackson plank went down to defeat, media pundits characterized it as a victory over "special inter-

ests"—meaning unions, blacks and allied groups. It could have been portrayed as a win *for* "special (wealthy) interests," but few mainstream journalists played it that way—certainly not the network TV news correspondents in high-income brackets themselves.

If Bill Clinton is the autumn foe of President Bush, even his faint populist noises will be taken to task. On "NBC Nightly News," correspondent Lisa Myers recently accused Clinton of practicing "class warfare" and of doing "an imitation of Walter Mondale, with unbridled appeals to special interests."

For the rest of the political campaign we'll be hearing plenty about rhetorical appeals for "class warfare." But major media don't necessarily object to class war—as long as it's being waged from the top down. It's the slightest hint of bottom-up stuff that gets the bad press.

April 22, 1992

The Takeover
of the Democratic Party

New York

Thousands of journalists covered the 1992 Democratic National Convention here. Almost all of them missed the biggest story.

The story wasn't missed because it happened in the shadows or in some smoke-filled back room. It was by-passed because of ideological blinders worn by so many in the conformist press.

The big story was the takeover of the Democratic Party by big business.

Of course, the Democratic Party has always included hefty doses of corporate interests. But the significance of this convention is that corporate America has taken undisputed control—at least for now—of both major political parties, not just the GOP.

How did so many in the political press corps miss the story? Most establishment journalists seem blind to the fact that corporations are thoroughly political institutions, seeking ever-increasing influence over parties, legislation and government regulation. (These businesses are, after all, the folks who underwrite the news with their advertising.)

In political reporting, corporations are treated as benign, neutral, invisible. Their political maneuvers are generally not news.

It's not that journalists are oblivious to political wheeling and dealing by various groups. In the days before and during the convention, political reporters scrutinized teachers' unions, black activists, senior-citizen groups, feminists, gay-rights advocates—denigrating them as "special interests" who could ruin "Clinton's convention" by "alienating middle-class voters."

Be True to Your Class: Corporate Spin

With so much media focus on these relatively power-less grassroots groups, powerful corporations—the country's *real* special interests—ran off with the party.

Item: Two days before the convention, a "Victory Train" carried congressional Democrats from Washington to New York. Accompanying the party elite on the train ride were corporate lobbyists who paid $10,000 to $25,000 for the right to mingle and schmooze. The Democratic National Committee has been raking in money from virtually every corporate interest needing a government favor. The message to anti-poverty or consumer-rights activists: No need for you to come on board. You can wait at the station.

Item: The Clinton-Gore ticket represents the seizure of the party hierarchy by the Democratic Leadership Council, which is typically euphemized in the media as a group of "moderate" Democratic politicians who want the party to "speak for the middle class." (Clinton and Gore were founders of the DLC; Clinton was its chair in 1990-91.) The problem is that the DLC has no middle-class constituents. It is bankrolled by—and speaks for—corporate America: Arco, Dow Chemical, Georgia Pacific, Martin Marietta, the Tobacco Institute, the Petroleum Institute, etc.

Item: Clinton became the media-designated "front-runner" in large part because he raised so much money early in the campaign. The cash didn't come from middle-class folks. As reported by *In These Times*, most of it came from conservative business interests: investment bankers, corporate lobbyists and Wall Street firms which fund both major political parties.

Item: Two of Clinton's key fund-raisers were Robert Barry, a longtime General Electric lobbyist, and Thomas H. Boggs Jr., who earns $1.5 million a year as a lawyer-lobbyist with the Washington firm of Patton, Boggs and Blow. Boggs' parents were members of Congress; his sister is media pundit Cokie Roberts. His law firm boasts a computer program that matches corporate donors with members of Congress who seek his help in raising money; a

match depends on what legislation is pending before Congress.

Item: The Boggs law firm also boasts partner Ron Brown, chair of the Democratic Party. Some pundits have suggested that since Brown is African-American, the Clinton-Gore ticket has less need of Jesse Jackson to mobilize the black vote in November. But Ron Brown is far more familiar with corporate boardrooms and government corridors than grassroots organizing. His clients have included an array of U.S. and foreign business interests, as well as the regime of Haitian dictator Jean Claude Duvalier.

When Jerry Brown spent his campaign denouncing "Washington sleaze," he was referring to these kinds of cozy corporate-government relations.

But mainstream media have demonstrated far less animus toward corporate influence than toward Jerry Brown, who was routinely described by journalists covering the convention as "disruptive," "egotistical" and a "party pooper."

Aided by this media slant, corporate insiders are laughing all the way to the bank.

July 15, 1992

The Privatization of Public TV

Arguments have been flying thick and fast about America's public TV network.

Attackers like Senators Jesse Helms and Bob Dole threaten to cut off funds to PBS, denouncing it as some kind of leftist hotbed. The claim makes for fiery rhetoric. The only trouble is, it's absurd.

Defenders of public TV don't exactly give the whole picture either. "There is no PBS political agenda to the left, right or center," network executive Robert Ottenhoff insists. Other news outlets depict PBS as a bastion of integrity. "Businesses underwrite certain productions, but shows aren't influenced by sponsors," Associated Press reported flatly.

The problem with this narrow debate is that both sides are wrong. PBS is neither a left stronghold nor an independent network free of bias and corporate influence.

Many PBS stations air three programs every week hosted by editors who hail from the right-wing *National Review* magazine: William F. Buckley's "Firing Line," plus a pair from the ubiquitous John McLaughlin, "One On One" and "The McLaughlin Group."

For years, PBS's weekly look at foreign affairs, "American Interests," has been hosted by foreign policy conservative Morton Kondracke. And the once-a-week PBS program aimed at blacks, "Tony Brown's Journal," is hosted by a Republican.

Meanwhile, PBS does not offer one weekly show hosted by an advocate of the left.

In programming on the economy, it's business as usual. PBS stations offer regular coverage of corporate news and agendas: "Adam Smith's Money World," "Wall $treet Week" hosted by conservative Louis Rukeyser, and the "Nightly Business Report." PBS does not offer a single weekly news/talk show presenting the agendas of groups often in conflict with big business, such as consumers, labor or environmentalists.

All the commotion from right-wing critics is about the tiny minority of PBS programming they find offensive: a dozen or so "leftist" documentaries per year. Given the conservative, pro-corporate bias in PBS's weekly lineup—several hundred programs per year—it could be argued there are far too few of such documentaries.

And PBS-bashing conservatives—who dismiss Bill Moyers' world class documentaries on our constitutional checks and balances as "propaganda"—never criticize PBS for airing unabashed agit-prop films produced by right-wing groups like Rev. Sun Myung Moon's political arm CAUSA, or the misnamed Accuracy In Media.

The bias in the weekly lineup would be easy to fix—by adding shows with hosts and agendas opposed to the Buckleys and Rukeysers. But PBS has not done this, and there's a simple reason: Big money talks as loudly on "noncommercial" public TV as on the avowedly commercial TV networks.

PBS officials admit their weekly current events lineup favors conservative commentators, but they say they can't find funding for an opposing show. In essence, corporate underwriters—such as the Wall Street firms that sponsor PBS's business shows—are determining which programs are seen, and which are not.

While corporate execs can often see themselves on PBS, it's another matter for working people. A City University of New York study found that PBS primetime coverage that "addressed the lives and concerns of workers as workers" totaled 27 hours in 1988 and 1989, less than half of one percent of its total primetime programming. And of those paltry 27 hours on working people, 19 were about British workers—leaving 20 minutes per month about U.S. workers.

PBS programs featuring tough critics of government or corporate policies—such as "The Kwitny Report"—have

Be True to Your Class: Corporate Spin

died for lack of funds. By contrast, Bill Buckley's "Firing Line" is so well-funded by corporations and conservative foundations that it could afford to pay Jack Kemp $30,000 for two guest appearances.

And what about the "MacNeil/Lehrer NewsHour," the crown jewel of PBS daily programming? A 1989 study commissioned by the media watch group FAIR, examining the show's guest list, found it dominated by government and corporate officials, but lacking in public interest advocates for civil rights, the environment, consumer rights, etc.

MacNeil/Lehrer repeatedly features scholars from conservative think tanks, but not progressive ones. With such an establishment-dominated guest list, it's no mystery why AT&T and Pepsico have sponsored the program to the tune of $12 million per year—half the entire Mac-Neil/Lehrer budget.

By harping on a handful of controversial documentaries, Jesse Helms and his allies hope to enforce a still more conservative slant at PBS. As usual in Washington debates, the key question isn't even being asked: If countries across Western Europe can have strong, diverse public broadcasting systems free of corporate influence, why can't we?

March 25, 1992

"Pro-Corporate Tilt" Polluting Media

Twenty years after passage of the Endangered Species Act, many Americans are hoping that President Clinton will stand behind such environmental laws—long undermined by previous administrations.

"For ourselves and future generations," Clinton's campaign platform declared, "we must protect our environment." Of course such pledges have been heard before.

The media's task of separating flowery rhetoric from policy realities is more crucial than ever. But when journalistic institutions cater to private business, they cannot safeguard public health.

Big media outlets are intertwined with—or owned outright by—huge corporations. A major toxic dumper and despoiler of waterways, General Electric, owns NBC. Other large firms are mega-buck investors in media, and frequently spend huge sums to advertise on the airwaves and in print.

Corporate power to distort environmental realities is typified by TV ads featuring merrily clapping seals—produced by DuPont, a leading chemical contaminator—and "plant a tree" ads from timber companies that clear-cut forests. (Chevron spent several hundred thousand dollars on an ad campaign hyping its butterfly preservation effort that cost the company $5,000 per year.)

On so-called "public TV," a dozen big corporate polluters—including BASF, Goodyear and Mobil—polish their images by underwriting nature shows. Environmentalists refer to these commercials and programs as *ecopornography.*

With an increasingly corporate atmosphere, newsrooms rarely produce sharp probes of the private sector. When news accounts do tell of serious pollution, white-collar swindles, dangerous consumer products and the like, the reporting usually lags behind government investigations and court indictments.

Even when companies literally get away with murder, news coverage of crime in the suites tends to be far less graphic—and far more skimpy—than coverage of crime in the streets.

"A built-in, chronic tilt chills mainstream press coverage of grave, persisting, and pervasive abuses of corporate power," contends Morton Mintz, who left the *Washington Post* in 1988 after 29 years as a reporter there.

For more than a third of a century, Mintz has aggressively reported on giant pharmaceutical companies, automakers, the tobacco industry and other manufacturers of hazardous products. His work has been conspicuous—because such intrepid journalism is so rare.

News media generally see themselves as watchdogs of government, but not of corporations. That, says Mintz, is a fatal journalistic flaw: "Underlying the pathetically inadequate coverage of life-threatening corporate misconduct is the everlasting embrace by the press of a truly absurd but wondrously convenient rationale for pro-corporate tilt: in an industrial society government constitutes the whole of governance."

As Mintz pointed out in Harvard's *Nieman Reports* in late 1991: "It is beyond doubt that the large corporation has always governed, most importantly by deciding whether untold numbers of people will live or die, will be injured, or will sicken."

The press has greatly improved since the early part of this century, according to Mintz, but today the stakes are much higher. "For decades now, the corporate potential to inflict bodily harm has been increasing rapidly, by reason of the onward march of perilous new technologies—chemical, nuclear, and others."

Rather than challenging this "onward march," some prominent journalists have jumped on the toxic bandwagon. Former CBS anchor Walter Cronkite set a bad example by narrating a pro-pesticide documentary, "Big Fears, Little Risks," which aired on PBS television stations in 1989.

Once called "the most trusted man in America," Cronkite earned $25,000 by reading a script that dismissed consumer fears of carcinogenic pesticides as "chemophobia." Under the sponsorship of the American Council on Science and Health, an industry-backed group, the film was indirectly funded by pesticide-makers Dow and Monsanto.

Corporate domination of news is accelerating via swift consolidation of media ownership. The latest evidence appears in the fourth edition of Ben Bagdikian's book *The Media Monopoly*. The new edition shows that about 20 corporations—down from 50 a decade ago—now reap most of the revenue from U.S. newspapers, magazines, TV, books and movies.

It's difficult for reporters (like any employees) to bite the hand that signs the paycheck, especially in tough economic times.

Morton Mintz has observed that journalists "learn what kind of reporting is wanted and rewarded. They also learn what kind is unwanted and discouraged—by, say, the editing of hard-hitting stories into mush, burial of page-one stories and recalls of unsafe consumer products in back pages, and denial of merit pay increases and promotions."

But Mintz does not attribute the pro-corporate slant to big media owners and managers alone: "Reporters do not deserve to get off so easily. Those who attempt serious coverage of corporate governance and misconduct often break through, even when they inflict pain on personal friends of the owners and managers. Too many reporters don't even try."

As we proceed into the Clinton era, don't expect in-depth media coverage of environmental degradation and other corporate misdeeds.

January 27, 1993

Part IV
Health and Safety

Warning: Mass media priorities may be hazardous to your health. The same news outlets featuring advice on how to be healthy are all too often—actively or passively—aiding injury and disease. How? With unhealthy doses of double standards, corporate coziness and overreliance on official viewpoints.

Journalism Lost in Smoke

Every once in a while, big media outlets criticize the cigarette industry. Then, like habitual puffers dashing out of smoke-free zones, they take evasive action.

The occasional media probes of tobacco are popgun assaults compared to the steady "war on drugs" barrage.

Cigarettes now kill 434,000 Americans each year, according to the federal Centers for Disease Control. Cocaine and crack claim 3,300 lives. But double standards pervade mass media.

A TV documentary, "48 Hours on Crack Street," inspired the weekly CBS program "48 Hours"—which returns regularly to the topic of illegal drugs. But out of the first 162 hour-long productions, only one dealt with cigarettes.

The Lorillard tobacco tycoon who owns CBS, Laurence Tisch, probably does not object to such priorities.

Tobacco interests maintain influence over broadcast media even without owning them. Federal law bars cigarette ads from the airwaves, but Philip Morris buys plenty of commercials for products like Miller Beer, Jell-O and Kool-Aid. As the country's third-largest advertiser on network TV, Philip Morris paid $390 million to ABC, CBS and NBC in 1991.

With its huge circulation—15 million copies per week—*TV Guide* could shine a bright light on network deference to a tobacco industry responsible for more than one in six American deaths. But the magazine won't touch the story with a ten-foot antenna.

As assistant managing editor Andrew Mills told us in 1989, "It wouldn't look good for *TV Guide* to go after the networks when *TV Guide* runs cigarette ads in every issue." In recent years the weekly has not printed a single article about television and tobacco.

Ironically, in a 1992 interview with us, *TV Guide* editor-in-chief Anthea Disney expressed concern about the impact of role models: "I wouldn't run a photo of a person smoking if I could help it." Yet *TV Guide* does so routinely—in colorful cigarette ads. And, the magazine brags to advertisers, more than 5 million teenagers thumb through its pages each week.

We've all seen fervent pleas by the Partnership for a Drug-Free America. Using ad space donated by mass media, the organization warns young people against marijuana, crack and cocaine—but never mentions cigarettes or alcohol. As it happens, the "Drug Free" partnership has some corporate funders that are anything but drug free, such as Philip Morris, Anheuser-Busch, and RJR Nabisco.

While RJR Nabisco helps bankroll save-the-kids-from-drugs ads, its subsidiary R.J. Reynolds keeps ignoring pleas to cancel massive Old Joe Camel advertising campaigns that are hooking children.

In the wake of findings that 6-year-olds are as familiar with the Camel's Old Joe cartoon character as with Mickey Mouse, U.S. Surgeon General Antonia Novello and the American Medical Association denounced the ad campaign and urged a halt to it. With the nation's children already smoking 947 million packs of cigarettes annually, the stakes are high.

Women also are special targets. In 1991 a half-dozen women's magazines—*Cosmopolitan, Family Circle, Glamour, Harper's Bazaar, Mademoiselle* and *Self*—raked in $27 million from cigarette advertisers.

Every month 12,000 American women die as a result of cigarettes. But *Cosmopolitan* editor Helen Gurley Brown is unapologetic that her magazine collected $8.6 million from cigarette ads last year—while staying away from articles about smoking. "I can't be interviewed on the subject of cigarettes," she told us last week.

Brown, whose glossy magazine includes nine pages of cigarette ads in its April 1992 issue, seems to be standing by her 1985 statement: "Having come from the advertising world myself, I think 'Who needs somebody you're paying millions of dollars a year to come back and bite you on the ankle?'"

An exhaustive study—published in the Jan. 30, 1992 issue of the *New England Journal of Medicine*—found "strong statistical evidence that cigarette advertising in magazines is associated with diminished coverage of the hazards of smoking. This is particularly true for magazines directed to women." As a result of the scarcity of independent journalism, "Americans substantially underestimate the dangers of smoking as compared with other risks to health."

Tobacco companies spend $3.2 billion a year on advertising in the United States. They are not only promoting their deadly product. They are also buying media silence.

Full-color cigarette ads keep rolling off the presses. Respiratory illnesses, cancer, and heart disease will come later, mentioned in plain black ink on obituary pages.

March 18, 1992

The Tobacco Industry's Smoke Screen

When CNN aired a recent news report about the political leverage of the tobacco industry, viewers caught a rare glimpse of a TV network probing the cigarette business.

A few key facts were damning.

- Nicotine-stained contributions to the two major parties have more than quadrupled in 1992 compared to 1988. During the first half of '92 the Democrats took in $731,000 from cigarette companies, and the Republicans almost twice as much—$1.34 million.

- "Thirteen Bush campaign officials, including Craig Fuller, have ties to tobacco," CNN explained. "Fuller managed the Republican convention, and is also a vice president of Philip Morris. Repeated efforts to contact the Bush Administration for a response were unsuccessful."

- The Clinton campaign, though less implicated, is hardly pure. Its chairperson, Mickey Kantor, is among three top Clinton staffers with tobacco links.

CNN correspondent Jeff Levine went beyond the data supplied by a pair of consumer groups. His report included an interview with a representative of the American Heart Association, who blamed "the political and economical clout of the tobacco industry" for the fact that "there has been absolutely no significant legislation passed in the United States Congress that would regulate this dangerous, addictive killer."

The study of the tobacco industry's bipartisan contributions, released in August 1992 by Public Citizen and the

Advocacy Institute, got only a smattering of other news coverage.

Days earlier, Anna Quindlen's opinion column in the *New York Times* had eloquently denounced "the enormous power of the tobacco lobby." But that lobby has friends in high media places. Including the *New York Times*.

When the U.S. government's trade representative moved to boost tobacco exports in 1989, a *Times* editorial expressed some regrets before concluding that it was "hard to object" to hawking U.S. cigarettes in the Third World. [A *New York Times* board member, Louis Gerstner, headed tobacco giant RJR Nabisco at the time.]

In another editorial the same day, however, the *Times* suddenly lost its tolerance for sellers of addictive substances: "America pays a terrible price for cocaine addiction."

Some drug trafficking, it seems, is more despicable than others.

September 2, 1992

AIDS Coverage:
Lives in the Balance

The person who jolted America's news media out of its lethargy about AIDS was no journalist. He was a movie idol.

Ten years ago the recorded cases of AIDS were rising steeply, but news coverage was minuscule. It remained that way even as scientific knowledge and alarm leapt in 1983 and 1984. The deadly illness didn't really hit the front pages and network news until 1985—the year it killed Rock Hudson.

A second big jump in AIDS stories came in 1987, mainly boosted by two factors: Liberace's death from the disease, and indications that heterosexual contact might put people at risk. Nightly network news reports on AIDS and HIV doubled from the previous year. So did print articles.

"The media are convinced in 1987 that they're doing a great job reporting the AIDS story, and there's no denying they've grasped the horror," Paul Monette wrote (in his book *Borrowed Time*) that year. "But for four years they let the bureaucrats get away with passive genocide, dismissing a no-win problem perceived as affecting only an underclass or two."

Monette did not mince words: "It was often remarked acidly in [the gay community of] West Hollywood that if AIDS had struck boy scouts first rather than gay men, or St. Louis rather than Kinshasa [Zaire], it would have been covered like nuclear war."

Has media coverage improved since then? Well, yes and no. Some better journalism has emerged to help dispel ignorance and prejudice. But few news outlets consistently convey a sense of urgency.

Although scientific journals have steadily increased their volume of AIDS-related articles, national news media have actually reduced the amount of coverage in recent years.

The quantity of reports about AIDS and HIV has never returned to its 1987 level on evening network TV news. And a computer-search of major print media for articles about AIDS shows that Rock Hudson-year levels were not matched for four years—until Magic Johnson's announcement that he was HIV-positive in late 1991.

Why does the AIDS story need to be about a superstar to get mega-media attention? Isn't the widespread presence of AIDS a big enough story on its own?

Some 160,500 AIDS deaths are already behind us in this country. The estimated global AIDS toll currently stands at over one million deaths. And for every person who has already died of AIDS, several others are now infected with the AIDS virus. Do we really need a celebrity diagnosis to make this epidemic a top media priority?

The fluctuating national news coverage—often delivered with a ho-hum tone—has given the impression to many that somehow the AIDS crisis has leveled off or even subsided. The opposite is true.

"We are all directly threatened...and we are all treating it like another news story," says Dr. Bruce Dan, a physician who is senior editor of the *Journal of the American Medical Association.* An Emmy Award-winning TV medical reporter, Dan blasts the journalistic profession for complacency on AIDS, which he calls "the biggest infectious-disease epidemic in the history of this planet."

Overall, news reporting conveys more a mood of routine than crisis. In short supply are hard-hitting stories about the lethal impacts of head-in-the-sand public policies.

As CBS News producer Rob Hershman puts it: "Once AIDS becomes another intractable social problem...it's background noise." He adds that "it takes personal passion to make background into foreground."

Hershman, who is HIV-positive, warns that "we're just not going to make it" if the burden of passionately tackling the AIDS story is left to gay reporters. "I'm tired. I'm sick," he says.

When covering AIDS, journalists should not use terms like "general population," "innocent victims" and "life-styles." Everyone is part of the general population. Nobody with AIDS is guilty. And "lifestyles" is another discounting buzzword that makes a gay sexual orientation sound somehow frivolous or cavalier.

Rather than utilize their tremendous power on behalf of public health, mass media have failed to communicate vital AIDS-prevention information. For example, the same national TV networks that use sexual titillation to sell everything from cars to whipped cream to their own programming have rejected condom commercials and explicit AIDS spots.

While stressing that *anyone* can acquire AIDS through high-risk activities like unprotected sex and sharing needles, news media should extensively cover demographic groups that are being ravaged by the disease—gay men, racial minorities, the poor.

We are all in this together. The news media must pull their weight.

December 2, 1992

A "Super Sunday"
for Domestic Violence

If you watch NBC's Super Bowl broadcast closely, amid the clutter of ads hawking Gillette razors, Nike sneakers and the like, you'll see one that isn't selling anything.

It's a public service spot, with a simple message, aimed at men: Beating your wife or girlfriend is a crime.

The ad should offer some solace to those who run shelters for battered women. Assuming they're not too busy to see it. Super Bowl Sunday is, after all, one of their worst days of the year.

For too many households, the violence of football's most-watched game spills from the gridiron into the home. The Super Bowl brings together many activities that can "trigger" a man predisposed to battering: intense viewing of sanctioned violence, heavy drinking, betting.

Women's shelters have reported big increases in calls for help on Super Bowl day. This year, some shelters may double their staff to prepare for the influx.

To say "Super Sunday" is a bad day for domestic violence is saying a lot. Consider what a "normal" day is like.

- An American woman is beaten in her home every 18 seconds.

- Each day, 3,000 domestic violence crimes against women are reported; as many as 10,000 more go unreported.

- Each day, domestic violence sends more women to emergency rooms than any other cause—more than auto accidents, muggings and rapes combined.

If this sounds like a year-round national crisis, why hasn't the battering epidemic been presented as such in big news outlets?

One reason is that national media take their cues on what is a national crisis from official Washington, as opposed to, say, directors of battered women's shelters or feminist leaders.

To the men who've run Washington and the national media in recent years, the crisis in American homes is drugs. "If this is a war," declared NBC's Tom Brokaw on the subject of drugs, "we're all soldiers. Not a war that can be won with more money alone, or just tougher laws, or better treatment. This is a test of our national will."

Like good soldiers, national media have marshalled their considerable resources against illegal drugs. All that's been raised against domestic violence is a white flag.

A National Newspaper Index search (1988-1990) revealed that for every article on domestic violence in leading dailies, there were eight on drugs. For every report on prevention of battering, there were 22 on prevention of drug use.

On editorial pages, drug use is the focus of impassioned concern, sometimes proclaimed the biggest problem facing the country. Domestic violence isn't proclaimed anything by editorial writers—it's hardly mentioned.

While journalists wage rhetorical war against the "drug scourge," language is much softer about batterers. Violent men are often written about in euphemisms—as participants in "a stormy relationship" or "a marriage gone sour."

From national media one wouldn't know that about as many Americans die from beatings in the home as from cocaine and crack.

The media's drumbeat aids "war on drugs" legislation. By contrast, the Violence Against Women Act introduced by Senator Joseph Biden—aimed at reducing domestic violence and sexual assault, and providing services for survivors—receives little media attention.

Last year's Super Bowl on CBS featured graphic anti-drug ads. This year's broadcast on NBC will address domestic violence—thanks to prodding from women's organizations and the media watch group FAIR (with which we are associated). The anti-battering message may well "save lives," says Denver psychologist Lenore Walker, who has written two books on domestic violence.

"When people view violence, they can become inured. It becomes easier for them to commit it," Walker observes. "The answer is not to ban TV violence, but to talk about it, bring it into the open, to defuse the connection between seeing violence and acting it out." Who better to bring such issues into the open than journalists?

Six years ago, *Mother Jones* magazine first linked the Super Bowl to domestic violence—followed by sports columnist Robert Lipsyte.

In 1990, Mike Capuzzo of the *Philadelphia Inquirer* examined the connection between viewing violent sports—football, basketball, hockey—and battering. (Watching nonviolent sports like baseball or tennis has no apparent impact.) He discovered that about 25 percent of the men seeking counseling to stop beating their wives had been violent after viewing sports.

On Jan. 31, the Super Bowl will come and go. And women's shelters will return to normal...with a woman beaten by her partner every 18 seconds.

Let's hope this year's Super Bowl wakes up national media to the epidemic of domestic violence.

January 20, 1993

Backlash: Some Journalists Still Discount Women

Shortly before "Super Sunday," we wrote a column breaking the news that NBC Sports would air a public service announcement against domestic violence during the Super Bowl's pre-game show. More people ended up watching the PSA than any anti-battering message in history.

Our column expressed hope that Super Bowl Sunday—an especially awful day for domestic violence—would be a wake-up call for the media on the long-underreported issue of battering.

At most media outlets, the wake-up call was heard loud and clear.

● On Super Sunday, *New York Times* columnist Robert Lipsyte recounted his visits to battered women's shelters in three states during the pro football playoffs of 1987: "Everybody involved was amazed at the similarity of experience across the nation: angry, frustrated men turning on their mates and children at the end of a game as if it were part of the ritual."

● The night after the game, "CBS Evening News" explored the link between the Super Bowl and domestic violence. An emergency room staffer in Dallas told CBS: "After all these sporting events, that's a prime time for the ladies to come in."

● The *Los Angeles Daily News* reported L.A. police statistics showing that felony domestic violence arrests had increased significantly on Super Bowl Sundays in 1991 and 1992. After this year's game, the paper noted: "Battered women shelters and hot lines in Los Angeles and Ventura counties reported twice the normal number of calls for help in the two days following the Super Bowl."

● Newspapers across the country quoted local shelter coordinators or beating victims telling of personal experiences. In Florida, a shelter director told the *St. Petersburg Times* of women who "try to make themselves scarce during Monday night football because their husband or boyfriend becomes dangerous and violent."

The strength of most of the reporting was its reliance on the real experts—the usually unsung heroes who run battered women's shelters and crisis lines for little or no pay. While many shelter directors told journalists that their busiest days were often linked to Super Bowls or other sporting events, some said they hadn't noticed such a link—that is, they assist battered and bruised women at a steady clip all year.

Another strength of the coverage was its emphasis on domestic violence as a *year-round* crisis. Many stories noted the shocking FBI statistic that a woman is beaten in the home every 18 seconds. Or the *Journal of the American Medical Association* finding that one-fourth to one-third of emergency room visits by women are linked to domestic violence.

Or the Senate Judiciary Committee report saying that our country has three times as many animal shelters as battered women shelters.

But while this year's Super Bowl was indeed a wake-up call for many media, a few journalists reacted by sleepwalking past the facts.

These journalists, mostly men, seemed to have a visceral reaction against all the attention being focused on domestic violence, and the link to football. "Where's the evidence?" they scoffed—as if the testimony of scores of women was irrelevant.

The "debunkers" claimed that a coalition of battered women's advocates and FAIR (the media watch group we work with) had misstated the facts in convincing NBC to run the Super Bowl ad. The problem with these "correct the record" reports is that their facts were often wrong.

They asserted that the coalition claimed "national studies" linked the Super Bowl to increased domestic violence. No such claims were made. That the coalition was forced to "acknowledge" its evidence was largely "anecdotal." There was nothing to *acknowledge* since "anecdotal" is the word the coalition had used in countless press interviews.

Although the *Washington Post* had focused only two front-page articles on the domestic violence crisis during the previous four years, that paper found space on its front page Super Bowl day for a "news" report—more like an editorial—attacking those who sought the NBC public service spot as "causists" who "show up wherever the most TV lenses are focused."

Ignoring firsthand accounts from women, *Post* reporter Ken Ringle wrote that "none of the activists appears to have any evidence that a link actually exists between football and wife-beating."

The *Post* article, which was reprinted in papers across the country, twisted facts and quotes. For example, one of the experts the *Post* cited to prove that "no evidence" links football and battering was Denver psychotherapist Michael Lindsey.

But the same day's *New York Times* quoted Lindsey as saying: "That PSA will save lives. It will give people the permission to call for help. The same way so much violence in football gives people permission to batter."

Confused? So were we.

When our associate Jim Naureckas called him, Lindsey said the *Post* reporter "was really hostile. He didn't want to talk about the larger issues... His whole focus was so far off the mark."

Relying heavily on the *Post* article, other outlets—including Associated Press, the *Boston Globe,* and syndicated columnist Alan Dershowitz—produced articles compounding the original inaccuracies. An error-filled *Wall Street Journal* editorial was contemptuous of battered women.

In her landmark book *Backlash,* Susan Faludi describes how progress toward equality for women often results in a journalistic backlash.

This Super Bowl, women finally had a hearing on domestic violence. It was too much for some journalists to accept.

February 10, 1993

As former President Reagan accepted an award in Las Vegas from the National Association of Broadcasters, a lone anti-nuclear protester disrupted the speech. This image, not the issue of nuclear testing, became the story.

Nuclear Testing:
The Media Non-Story

Las Vegas

Several thousand people gathered in the Nevada desert near here to demand an end to nuclear testing. Only one of them was deemed newsworthy by the national media.

The one considered news was the individual who—acting alone and foolishly—smashed a crystal trophy next to Ronald Reagan at a Las Vegas podium and sent glass flying...and news cameras popping.

As usual, the action photo replaced the deeper issue.

Only days earlier the French government had announced suspension of its 32-year nuclear testing program in the South Pacific. France offered to make the testing halt permanent if other nations reciprocate. "We will see," declared President Francois Mitterrand, "if our example is followed and if common sense is advanced."

Last year eight nuclear bombs exploded under the Nevada desert floor—half of them far more powerful than the atomic bombs that devastated Hiroshima and Nagasaki. The White House relies on news media to keep U.S. underground tests out of sight and out of mind.

Russia's government has reaffirmed Mikhail Gorbachev's moratorium on test explosions. That leaves the U.S. and China as the only countries where nuclear bombs explode.

In China, protests against nuclear testing are illegal and dangerous. In our country, such protests are legal—only the national media don't acknowledge their existence.

Many times in recent years, thousands of protesters have journeyed to Nevada to call for a comprehensive test ban. Media coverage outside the region is usually nil.

Again, in 1992, despite days of articulate and creative

nonviolent demonstrations in the Las Vegas area, there had been no national media coverage by April 13 when hundreds of protesters began a 60-mile march to the test site.

But hours later, when a lone activist smashed Reagan's glass trophy, suddenly national media found an anti-testing protest worth reporting. Footage and photos of the incident at the podium—where the former president was receiving an award from the National Association of Broadcasters—made big news.

"Surveys show that up to 70 percent of Americans would favor a comprehensive test ban," says Stephanie Fraser, an organizer of the anti-testing campaign in Nevada. "But the media don't want to talk about the fact that the government is still testing weapons out here."

When they do mention U.S. nuclear tests, major news outlets have routinely echoed official rationales for continuing them. In 1985, when Gorbachev launched the first of several unilateral Soviet test moratoriums, CBS News dismissed the initiative as "posturing" and "propaganda." The *New York Times* and *Los Angeles Times* didn't even headline the moratorium—but instead featured a quickie, spin-control response by President Reagan inviting Soviet observers to a Nevada nuclear test.

Soon came the editorials. The *New York Times* sneered at the moratorium as "a cynical propaganda blast" that "would ring hollow even if it had not come after an energetic series of Soviet test explosions." (In reality, the Soviet testing pace that year lagged behind the U.S. rate.) The *Washington Post* defended the administration's rejectionism in an editorial titled "Nuclear Tests Are Necessary."

In October 1991, reporting yet another U.S. refusal to join a Kremlin testing halt, CBS News anchor Bob Schieffer used the term "we" several times, declaring that "we" have long opposed a test moratorium. Since CBS owns no nuclear weapons, it's clear he was speaking for the U.S. government. So much for separation of press and state.

Among the demonstrators who keep returning to Nevada is Anthony Guarisco, the 64-year-old director of the Alliance of Atomic Veterans. Guarisco was among 300,000 U.S. troops exposed to aboveground nuclear weapons tests at close range between 1945 and 1962.

"Ten years ago, we were in the news when all we talked about was the atomic veterans trying to get into VA hospitals," Guarisco told us. "Now that we're opposing nuclear tests, the national media don't even approach us."

While news media bemoan the imminent acquisition of nuclear bombs by other nations, one of our country's dirty secrets is that continued nuclear testing undermines the Nuclear Non-Proliferation Treaty—which two decades ago committed nuclear powers to good-faith negotiations toward a full test ban. The U.S. is the world's leading violator of the treaty.

Few nations are likely to be convinced that they should rein in their nuclear weapons research while the United States keeps delivering its arrogant message—"Do as we say, not as we do"—every time the Nevada desert shakes with another nuclear explosion.

But national media seem as oblivious to the events at the Nevada Test Site as the gamblers who fill the Las Vegas casinos an hour's drive away.

[In October 1992, George Bush grudgingly signed a loophole-ridden law that could phase out U.S. nuclear tests by the end of 1996.]

April 15, 1992

Part V
Now It Can Be Told

Timing makes all the difference. Reported promptly, a journalistic exposé can change the course of history. Reported long after the events, an exposé is a footnote to history. Too much of today's "investigative journalism" is belated reporting of scandalous facts that were never publicized in time to make a difference.

Now It Can Be Told...
Years Too Late

"Now It Can Be Told!"

With these words, tabloid journalist Geraldo Rivera opened his nightly TV program taking a (usually lurid) look back at old stories, scandals and supposed coverups.

The carnival-like slogan suggested that no one but the crusading Geraldo was able to pry open some secret that had been kept sealed.

Recently, one of TV's most influential journalists, Ted Koppel, seemed to be imitating Geraldo with his own "Now It Can Be Told" special. The program—produced with *Newsweek* magazine—looked back at the July 1988 shootdown of an Iranian civilian airliner over the Persian Gulf by an American warship, the USS *Vincennes*.

Don't get us wrong. Koppel's "Nightline" special was solid journalism, exposing that most of what the Reagan Administration told the U.S. public and the world about the shootdown—which killed 290 civilians—was half-truths and lies.

The U.S. government version: The plane was outside the commercial air corridor, heading at high speed directly for the *Vincennes*, which was located in international waters.

As "Nightline" showed, this claim was false on all counts: The Iranian Airbus was well within the civilian corridor, climbing up and turning slowly away from the *Vincennes*, which was cruising inside Iran's territorial waters.

The special contained a video clip of Vice President George Bush presenting the U.S. position to the world at the United Nations: "This tragic accident...occurred in the midst of a naval attack initiated by Iranian vessels against a neutral vessel and subsequently against the *Vincennes* when she came to the aid of the innocent ship in distress."

As Koppel commented about Bush's U.N. performance: "Much, if not most, of what you just heard was
untrue. But that was certainly the party line." It wasn't the
Iranians who provoked the fighting that day. The U.S. did.

"Nightline" blamed the 290 civilian deaths not on the
ship captain's wrong split-second decision, but on the
Reagan Administration's secret policy that had placed U.S.
warships at risk by making the U.S. a de facto military ally
of Iraq in its war against Iran.

Given such tough, independent journalism by
"Nightline," why take a cheap shot at Koppel by comparing
him to Geraldo? Because a "Now It Can Be Told" special
today does not excuse the fact that "Nightline" reporting in
the days after the shootdown was little more than recycling
of White House deceptions.

Today, Koppel talks disdainfully of a Reagan Administration "party line." At the time, his show was a key
disseminator of that line. Indeed, most of the "facts" debunked by this month's special were dutifully reported as
true in July 1988 by "Nightline" journalists.

"Nightline" coverage in the wake of the U.S.
shootdown was light (a mere two-and-a-half programs)
and bland. Only Iranians could be heard expressing outrage
about the loss of life. It appeared unthinkable that the U.S.
government might be lying or should suffer international
sanctions.

Coverage was very different at "Nightline" five years
earlier when the U.S.S.R. shot down a Korean airliner over
Soviet territory. Then the outrage and calls for retribution
were instantaneous. Ted Koppel declared there wasn't
"any question that the Soviet Union deserves to be accused
of murder, it's only a question of whether it's first degree or
second degree."

In eight consecutive September 1983 programs on the
Soviet shootdown—the most intense single-story focus on
"Nightline" since the show was born in 1980 out of the Iran

hostage crisis—Koppel featured a steady parade of administration hawks and right-wing ideologues to denounce the Soviets. These included Jesse Helms ("premeditated, deliberate murder"), John Lofton ("sever diplomatic relations with the Soviet Union"), and Jeane Kirkpatrick ("the underlying cause of the whole thing was the Soviet proclivity for using violence, and then lying about it").

On one show, Koppel promoted a phone poll asking viewers whether the administration "should take strong action against the Soviets." Over 90 percent said yes.

The point here is that establishment journalists like Koppel don't wait years to challenge official misconduct…if the offending party is the Soviet Union or Iraq or Iran. But when the U.S. is the active or aggressive party in foreign affairs, don't hold your breath waiting for the national media to separate fact from fiction.

Ted Koppel is hardly unique as a practitioner of "Now It Can Be Told" journalism—parroting the official line until the truth is less threatening to the powers-that-be.

It took nine months before CBS "60 Minutes" revealed that hundreds of civilians were killed—many incinerated as they slept—in the early hours of the 1989 U.S. invasion of Panama. The story had been told within days of the invasion throughout Latin America and elsewhere.

During the first half of 1992, "Nightline" and other major news outlets got around to reporting on the Bush Administration's role in building up Saddam Hussein's financial and military power. The *Village Voice* ran the essence of that story on its cover—"Gulfgate: How the U.S. Secretly Armed Iraq"—in December 1990, a month before the war began.

When the next foreign war or invasion comes, most mainstream journalists can be counted on to swallow official deceptions. Months or years later, these news outlets may report the truth. But by then, the blood has been shed.

July 8, 1992

Journalism: What Went Wrong?

Last fall two journalists asked a difficult question—"America: What Went Wrong?"—and answered it with a stunning nine-part series in the *Philadelphia Inquirer*. Their work exposed a pattern of tax breaks and legalized corporate looting that stood Robin Hood on his head during the 1980s.

Readers were enthralled. About 20,000 contacted the newspaper about the series, written by *Inquirer* reporters Donald L. Barlett and James B. Steele. Across the country, daily papers reprinting the in-depth articles met with similar enthusiasm.

The response refuted a hollow management formula that has swept the newspaper industry—making articles shorter and shallower. As Barlett and Steele later observed, "readers want detailed information they can get nowhere else." They don't need to be spoon-fed news items chopped into little pieces like baby food—"they will read long stories if the material is interestingly written and appropriately presented."

Now, with a book version with the same title selling swiftly from coast to coast, we would do well to ask a parallel question—"Journalism: What Went Wrong?"

Throughout the 1980s, with few exceptions, media sentinels at the gates of power were snoozing—or nuzzling up to the White House. A month after Ronald Reagan moved in, the influential *New York Times* columnist James Reston declared that the Reagan economic program added up to a "serious attempt...to spread the sacrifices equally across all segments of society."

As the decade's giveaways to the wealthy grew more extreme, journalistic jargon muddied the waters. News media often called tax breaks for the affluent "tax reform." The situation became so absurd that the press sometimes described advocates of higher taxes for the rich as enemies of "reform."

In spring 1989, when a Gallup/Times-Mirror poll showed most of the U.S. public in favor of raising taxes on the well-to-do, the *International Herald Tribune* cited the survey as an indication of "anti-reform rumblings."

Some journalists—usually far from the corridors of power in Washington—did work to illuminate the economic realities of the 1980s as events unfolded. But their exceptional stories were overshadowed by the dominant spin. And when certain themes stay at the top of the news, off-key articles on the back pages have little impact.

"Every journalist knows that a story on the front page or its television equivalent can interest the whole country, but that the same story, inside, often has no impact at all," A.M. Rosenthal acknowledged in a *New York Times* column a few years ago. Rosenthal didn't mention that when he was executive editor of the *Times* during most of the Reagan era, he wielded enormous power to decide which stories would "interest the whole country" and which would have "no impact at all."

The savings-and-loan disaster is a case in point. The *Times* and other leading newspapers reported warning signs year after year during the mid-1980s—but usually far from front pages. One survey, by the *Chicago Media Critic* newsletter, concluded: "More than 85 percent of all the S&L stories we saw in the papers we monitored were hidden in the business sections."

Meanwhile, the front pages routinely trumpeted an economic boom. When the White House spewed out non-stop verbiage about "continuous economic expansion," few journalists questioned the hype.

Months after Reagan retired to California, the House Ways and Means Committee came out with a report that the *New York Times* summarized this way: "From 1979 to 1987 the standard of living for the poorest fifth of the population fell by 9 percent. At the same time, the living standard of the top fifth rose by 19 percent." The *Times* account

NOW, ABOUT EXTENDING THESE UNEMPLOYMENT BENEFITS--I'M *AGAINST* IT! GOVERNMENT HANDOUTS--DON'T *BELIEVE* IN 'EM! SELF-RELIANCE-- *THAT'S* THE SOLUTION!

AH, MR. PRESIDENT--

--SIR, SINCE THE WHITE HOUSE PRESS CORPS IS COMPRISED OF A BUNCH OF *WEENIES* AFRAID OF OFFENDING YOU AND POSSIBLY LOSING THEIR POSITIONS OF *PRIVILEGE*, I GUESS *I'LL* HAVE TO ASK THE OBVIOUS QUESTION--

--IF YOU ARE UNTROUBLED BY A $200 BILLION S+L BAILOUT AND A $70 BILLION FDIC BAILOUT--BOTH NECESSITATED BY THE *GREED* AND *MISMANAGEMENT* OF YOUR REPUBLICAN *CRONIES*--

--*WHY* DO YOU BALK AT SPENDING A *FRACTION* OF THAT TO HELP *AMERICANS IN NEED*?

COULD IT BE THAT YOU *DO* BELIEVE IN GOVERNMENT HANDOUTS--BUT ONLY FOR THE *RICH*?!

WELL, I--UH--*ahem!*

WHAT PAPER DID YOU SAY YOU'RE WITH?

©'91 TOM TOMORROW

quickly added a laughable understatement before it left the front page, explaining that "the Reagan Administration was not entirely free of responsibility for the change."

The *Times* article concluded by absolving those in power: "The actions of free markets and free people drove a giant wedge in the income distribution. Government responded by not responding, in effect leaving the rich and the poor to fend for themselves." In other words, the rich and poor were equally free to sleep under bridges and steal bread.

For many media heavyweights, the widening economic inequities weren't a big deal until conservative political analyst Kevin Phillips sounded the alarm a couple years ago with his book *The Politics of Rich and Poor.* By then, of course, immense damage had been done.

Journalists often seem to consider their job done when they show people suffering from economic deprivation. But showing dire circumstances does not necessarily explain how they came to pass, or help change them.

By documenting key causes of the economic debacle as well as its human consequences, Donald Barlett and James Steele lucidly explained events in terms of "why" as well as "what." Their revelations, however, came largely after the fact.

If Napoleon were still alive, he might repeat his comment that it's not necessary to censor the news—it's sufficient to delay the news until it no longer matters. So far, mainstream American journalism seems unable to probe the maneuvers of the power elite early enough to make much of a difference.

July 22, 1992

Delayed Response:
The Story of Brett Kimberlin

This is a tale of two newspapers named "Times"—one with enormous circulation and influence, the other small and unpretentious.

The *New York Times* waited three years to shed light on a scandal of major proportions: A federal prisoner, Brett Kimberlin, was thrown into solitary confinement a few days prior to the 1988 presidential election, after going public with his claim of having frequently sold marijuana to Dan Quayle.

The other newspaper, the weekly *Legal Times* in Washington, D.C.—with 10,000 subscribers, mostly lawyers—broke the essence of the story just six weeks after the events in a well-documented exposé published on December 19, 1988.

The *New York Times* finally printed a solid news article about the scandal on May 3, 1992. Most of it could have been written three years earlier.

The crux of the Kimberlin affair is not whether Quayle actually bought pot while a law student during the early 1970s. The issue is whether the U.S. Bureau of Prisons was used for political purposes by top Bush-Quayle campaign officials in the closing days of the 1988 presidential race.

The scrappy *Legal Times* indicated as much back in December 1988 with an extensive front-page article by investigative journalist Aaron Freiwald. But, with a few fleeting exceptions, the mass media slept on the story for three years.

They were rudely awakened in November 1991 by Garry Trudeau, a cartoonist who does extensive research before picking up a pen. Only after "Doonesbury" highlighted the Kimberlin case did major media begin to pay much attention.

Doonesbury

BY GARRY TRUDEAU

It was a long time coming, but the recent *New York Times* article could mark a turning point in media coverage of what was done to Brett Kimberlin, a 38-year-old prisoner who claims to have sold marijuana to Quayle at least a dozen times when Quayle was a law student in Indianapolis. Journalists should pursue questions such as these:

Has Kimberlin become a de facto political prisoner?

Kimberlin has been kept inside a federal penitentiary, despite his exemplary prison record, after having already served several more years than the eight-year maximum recommended in federal guidelines for a prisoner in his category. A May 10, 1992 "Doonesbury" Sunday comic strip featured a fictional reporter questioning a feathery Dan Quayle more rigorously than real-life journalists ever have:

"Mr. Vice President…a federal appeals court is scheduled to consider Brett Kimberlin's case. As you know, Kimberlin says he was thrown into solitary confinement to prevent him from talking about your DEA file and his own claims that he sold you marijuana. The federal Parole Commission then added five years to his recommended sentence…even though Kimberlin is a model prisoner with an extraordinary number of official commendations and degrees earned in prison. Sir, have you lost any sleep over what has been done to this man simply because of what he wanted to say about you?"

Has a federal prosecutor in Indianapolis used his office politically to fend off drug allegations against Quayle?

A new exposé published by *Legal Times* on March 30, 1992, stated: "Last November, the prosecutor, John Thar, brought an internal Justice Department investigation on himself by sharing Drug Enforcement Administration reports with the press. The inside information served to douse renewed speculation about a DEA probe into charges that Quayle had used cocaine in 1982.

"Two months later, Thar, an assistant U.S. attorney for the Southern District of Indiana, sent a letter to the U.S. Parole Commission that could delay the release of a federal prisoner [Kimberlin] who has been promoting his claim that he was Quayle's marijuana supplier in college."

Did leading operatives in the 1988 Bush-Quayle campaign, including James Baker, misuse the federal prison system for partisan purposes?

By *Legal Times'* undisputed account, Baker was repeatedly briefed during the last days of the '88 campaign about what Brett Kimberlin was doing and what was being done to him. The information came via the U.S. Bureau of Prisons and the Justice Department.

So far few Americans know about Baker's involvement. But British newspaper readers learned of it six months ago, when a *Guardian* article—headlined "Top officials implicated in Quayle drug case 'cover-up'"—began by describing "an extraordinary court case which could involve the secretary of state, James Baker."

In November 1991, awakened from its slumber by the pen-pricks of Garry Trudeau, the *New York Times* ran a belated editorial about Brett Kimberlin, headlined: "Was This Prisoner Silenced?" Yes, he was. And so, for too long, was most of the press.

May 13, 1992

A Prisoner
and the Play-It-Safe Press

Four days before the 1988 election—just prior to a scheduled press conference about his claim of having been Quayle's pot dealer—prison inmate Brett Kimberlin was put in solitary isolation. The unprecedented order came directly from the U.S. Bureau of Prisons director in Washington.

For a long time, these events were known to few Americans.

Fast forward to October 1992. What a difference four years can make.

This month Brett Kimberlin has been featured in magazines ranging from *The New Yorker* to *People*. The *New York Times* put his case on the front page. He appeared on NBC's "Today Show" via satellite. CNN did an in-depth report on how the U.S. Justice Department secretly taped his phone conversations with attorneys in an effort to discredit the allegations against Quayle.

Federal officials violated their own rules when they threw Kimberlin into "the hole" days before Bush was elected president. In addition, Kimberlin is to remain locked up until February 1994—despite an exemplary prison record—on orders of the presidentially-appointed U.S. Parole Commission. The 180 months of incarceration would be twice the maximum time recommended in federal guidelines (64-92 months) for a prisoner in his classification.

Big media institutions have finally begun giving the Kimberlin case the scrutiny it deserves. But most of the information was available years ago. What took them so long?

Blame it on the routines of mainstream journalism:

Reliance on official sources

When the weekly journal *Legal Times* published a page-one story in December 1988 outlining the extraordinary steps taken by the nation's prison director to muzzle Kimberlin on the eve of the election, major media didn't follow up. *New York Times* reporter Michael Wines wrote a watered-down and evasive summary of the *Legal Times* exposé, and then dropped the story. In 1989, when we asked him why, Wines explained that he had checked with some official sources—and concluded, without talking to Kimberlin, that the prisoner was just "a publicity hound."

Discounting the powerless

Many journalists erred when they assumed that the account from a prisoner alleging mistreatment was less credible than the claims of Justice Department officials.

Since someone else broke the story, it's not so important.

The impressive *Legal Times* exposé merited further coverage back in late 1988. But mainstream journalists steered clear. National Public Radio's legal affairs reporter, Nina Totenberg, offers a dubious explanation: "We didn't think it was enough of a story—it was in a legal publication—to merit a follow-up."

Avoiding complicated stories.

The Kimberlin case is complex, and few journalists have done much to unravel it. One magazine that deserves credit for telling the story in stunning detail is *The New Yorker*. Staff writer Mark Singer concludes his 22,000-word piece in the Oct. 5, 1992 issue with a quotation from Erwin Griswold, former dean of the Harvard Law School and former U.S. solicitor general under Presidents Johnson and Nixon. Griswold says of Kimberlin: "In substance, he has become a political prisoner." Read Singer's article and you'll understand why.

Playing it safe

In autumn 1990, *People* magazine flew a reporter and an editor to a Memphis prison, where they spent five hours interviewing Kimberlin. The magazine sat on the story for two years—declining to publish a word about him until October 1992.

When cartoonist Garry Trudeau dramatized the Kimberlin story in his "Doonesbury" comic strip in late 1991, big-ticket journalists who knew nothing about Kimberlin were quick to slam the well-informed Trudeau as irresponsible.

Meanwhile, in federal court, Kimberlin won the right to a trial in his lawsuit charging false imprisonment, illegal wiretapping and denial of his First Amendment rights by Reagan-Bush officials.

If all the belated media attention had come earlier, Brett Kimberlin might be outside prison walls today. And even now, there is no guarantee that mainstream news media will probe the irregular parole rulings that keep him behind bars.

Journalism, like freedom, is a constant struggle.

October 21, 1992

Part VI
Press and Prejudice

Major news media love to tell us what a great pluralistic society we have. But they are far less adept at reflecting diversity on their pages or airwaves. Mainstream reporters and commentators often discuss groups of people who rarely speak for themselves in mass media. As a result, big media institutions are awash in ideological, racial, and cultural biases.

Media Hypocrisy
on Political Correctness

The "politically correct" uproar has gained an enormous amount of ink and air time recently. But the profuse warnings against a clear and present PC danger have left unmentioned the nation's most powerful arbiters of political correctness—the news media.

The very institutions sounding the loudest alarms against political correctness are the ones with the most clout to routinely define America's politically acceptable boundaries. A few executive producers at TV networks and top editors for key print media have incomparably more to say about what ideas will or won't reach the American people than all the campus activists in the country put together.

What we get when we turn on our televisions for news or public affairs programs is usually akin to white noise: constant and familiar, with little variation. The prevailing pundits—heard in sound bites or as panelists—are as predictable as the soundtrack of a TV test-pattern before dawn. The limits of their droning discussions, and the day-to-day exclusions of divergent voices, define political correctness.

The problem extends well beyond commercial broadcasting. Public TV's highly-touted "MacNeil/Lehrer NewsHour" has a guest list that is exceedingly confined. A FAIR study documented that NewsHour coverage of international affairs featured American guests who were 94 percent white and 94 percent male. What's more, 67 percent were present or former U.S. government officials; the remaining third included many academics and think-tankers closely aligned with Washington policy-makers. Arguments can run hot and heavy, while remaining within narrow bounds.

The fact is that a paucity of diverse outlooks is routine on network TV. In short, with few exceptions, the guests are limited to those whose views are politically correct—as far as the media powers-that-be are concerned.

Lately the PC establishment has been busily pointing fingers elsewhere, particularly at campuses. A single *Newsweek* column by George Will described PC villains five different times as "radicals," a codeword for political incorrectness if ever there was one. This is typical whiplash: The more that pundits flog the PC horse, the more their own hysteria—and intolerance—gain momentum. And along the way, rigorous limits on public discourse remain in force without challenge.

"The great triumphs of propaganda have been accomplished, not by doing something, but by refraining from doing," Aldous Huxley observed. "Great is truth, but still greater, from a practical point of view, is silence about truth."

A litmus test for political correctness—and a prerequisite for season tickets around the mass media's punditry table—is demonstrated and reliable silence about matters that the real PC enforcers do not want seriously addressed. "Radicals" need not apply.

America's grandest media institutions operate as if hosting an immense—and rigged—game of Jeopardy: with prepared answers that won't lead to crucial questions. Reporting on federal policies rarely illuminates the vested interests and leverage that mega-corporations maintain. When the United States went to war with Iraq, for example, the profits for U.S. arms makers received little coverage by big media—including NBC, which is owned by General Electric, a huge Pentagon contractor.

Media powerhouses—whose boards routinely overlap with the directors of banks and other top financial institutions—prefer not to acknowledge the impacts of corporate magnates, including their owners, as current events unfold. While claiming to inform and elucidate, the most powerful purveyors of "information" are frequently about mystifying who controls what, why, and how.

As a result we are inundated with what political scientist Paul N. Goldstene has called "a view of the world which controls perceptions of what is, and limits the possibilities of what might be." We continuously meet power "concentrated and screened from perception which it increasingly constructs"; we are moving to "a condition where the effects of power are pervasive, but where its identity is lost."

Multicultural openness is essential to truly democratic discourse: the inclusion of voices and vantage points too often filtered out of mass-mediated public life in America. The PC status quo, however, is much more interested in maintaining its media dominance.

When George Will fulminates against "instruments of indoctrination" that promote "officially approved thinking," he's not complaining about the indoctrination process that keeps him on network TV every week while keeping "radical" critics off. Pleased to equate don't-rock-the-boat positions with the essence of reasoned thought, the media's preeminent definers of political correctness give short shrift to anyone with a different definition.

Decades ago the journalist A.J. Liebling observed that "freedom of the press is guaranteed only to those who own one." Today we might add that the most sweeping power to suppress "politically incorrect" opinion is exercised by the mass media, even while they denounce political correctness as an ominous threat to freedom.

June 30, 1991

Is Anti-Arab Bigotry
Acceptable to News Media?

If a former U.S. secretary of state flatly declared that "you can't really believe anything an Arab says," would that be big news?

Or are we so accustomed to anti-Arab prejudices that this statement by Henry Kissinger—first publicized in the article you're now reading—won't be considered newsworthy?

Time will tell.

We have obtained a tape recording of Kissinger's comment, made at a fund-raising event which the *New York Times* termed an "Israel benefit."

Kissinger, who sits on the CBS board of directors, was joined in the panel discussion by two prominent CBS News employees—anchor Dan Rather and Middle East analyst Fouad Ajami, described by Rather that evening as "a very long-time CBS News consultant, one of our in-house wise men."

But neither the anchor nor the "in-house wise man" uttered a word of objection when—during the $250-a-plate dinner in New York City for the Jerusalem Foundation on June 3, 1992—Kissinger seemed to render his verdict against an entire ethnic group.

Imagine if a former secretary of state had publicly declared, "You can't really believe anything a Jew says." Or, "You can't really believe anything a black says." It's hard to believe the CBS News anchor would have let such a statement pass without challenge.

But among the many U.S. news outlets with a routinely anti-Arab tone, one of the most flagrant is "CBS Evening News"—where the task of denigrating Palestinians and other Arabs often falls to a man considered by many Arab-Americans to be the equivalent of an Uncle Tom, the

Lebanese-born academic Fouad Ajami.

At the Jerusalem Foundation event, Ajami drew laughs by making fun of Bedouin Arabs. He belittled the Palestinian cause, and repeatedly proclaimed that Arabs were incapable of practicing democracy.

Ajami explained his participation in the Israel benefit with these words: "I was simply drafted for this assignment by two people I can never say 'no' to, and that's Marty Peretz and Mort Zuckerman." Ajami was expressing an affinity with two of the most fervent Israel-can-do-no-wrong magnates in the media: Peretz of *The New Republic* and Zuckerman of *U.S. News and World Report.*

Kissinger's ethnic slur that night may have raised few eyebrows in the room because it was in sync with the tenor of the entire evening.

Peretz led off by lauding Kissinger and Ajami: "No two men have taught us more clearly...the unflinching hard realities of the Middle East than our two speakers today." Then, to loud applause, Peretz praised Dan Rather—"the moderator, the chairman, really, of this evening"—as "my favorite newsman."

More than 10,000 words of unmitigated praise for Israel followed, along with recurring mockery of Arabs. Martin Peretz's "favorite newsman" took turns with Kissinger and Ajami in playing to the prejudices of the audience.

Dan Rather said that "many of us celebrate" 25 years of Jerusalem "united under Israeli rule." He didn't mention the numerous U.N. Security Council resolutions declaring Israel's annexation of Palestinian East Jerusalem illegal.

Why didn't Rather object to Kissinger's assertion that "you can't really believe anything an Arab says"? Perhaps the explanation has to do with the attitudes that prevail at his work place. To watch the "CBS Evening News" is to see the Middle East through the eyes of Israel. And in that world view, Palestinian people look very small and far away.

But they don't look that way to our associate at the

media watch group FAIR, Sam Husseini, who discovered the Kissinger comments on a tape of the Jerusalem Foundation event. Husseini, a Palestinian-American, was deeply offended: "I thought we'd progressed beyond the point where it was acceptable to declare an entire people untrustworthy."

Along with asking why Rather remained silent about Kissinger's anti-Arab remark, the public should also ask what he was doing on the dais in the first place—at an event where some of the money raised will help settle immigrants on Israeli-occupied territory.

As Rather has demonstrated in the past, a journalist claiming to be objective will lose credibility when he or she becomes a cheerleader in a foreign conflict. That's what happened when Rather became an enthusiastic advocate for the Afghan rebels in the 1980s. "CBS Evening News," where Rather is managing editor, was shown to have aired false reports, phony battle footage and accounts of nonexistent victories by anti-government guerrillas.

If Dan Rather is so eager to line up with chronic Arab-bashers, that's his prerogative. But perhaps in the future his reports on the Middle East should be labeled "commentary."

And perhaps the news media of this country will tell Henry Kissinger that he owes Arab people an apology.

July 29, 1992

CBS Sees No Problem
with Anti-Arab Attitudes

CBS doesn't get it.

Two weeks ago, this column made public an ugly comment by former Secretary of State Henry Kissinger: "You can't really believe anything an Arab says." Since then a controversy has developed, reverberating in newspapers from the *Washington Post* and *Toronto Star* to the *Jerusalem Post*. Much of the uproar has centered on CBS anchor Dan Rather, who led the panel discussion at the Jerusalem Foundation benefit dinner in New York where Kissinger—a CBS board member—made his comments.

Dan Rather, who let Kissinger's statement pass without objection, now seems almost clueless about the reasons his own conduct is being challenged.

His failure to question the bigoted statement by fellow panelist Kissinger is only part of the problem. He also didn't object when another panelist, CBS News Middle East analyst Fouad Ajami, made derogatory comments about Arabs—and repeatedly insisted that Arabs are incapable of democracy.

Another issue is Rather's participation in an event billed as an "Israel benefit" that raised funds to help Jewish immigrants settle in the occupied territory of East Jerusalem. Israeli control of Palestinian East Jerusalem is deemed illegal by the U.N. Security Council and the United States.

Amazingly, Rather told Knight-Ridder reporter Marc Gunther that he didn't realize the Jerusalem Foundation, which supports Israel's occupation of East Jerusalem, "could be considered a partisan group."

Dan Rather still seems unaware that his role in the June 3 fundraiser—including his celebratory remarks about Jerusalem "unified under Israeli rule" and his comment that the city is threatened by an Arab "population explosion"—

makes him appear to be an advocate for Israeli policies.

What's more, Rather may have violated internal CBS guidelines for news employees, which we've obtained. The *CBS News Standards* manual states: "Employees who, in their private capacity, take a public position on a controversial issue…will either be removed from handling the news involving that issue or be required to take a leave of absence. The rationale behind this policy is that an employee who takes such a public position loses, at a minimum, the *appearance* of objectivity." (Emphasis in original.)

There's been quite a loss in Rather's "appearance of objectivity" during the past couple of weeks. But that doesn't seem to worry his boss at CBS.

"Comments made by individuals in their personal capacity are not the responsibility of CBS News," declared the president of CBS News, Eric W. Ober, in an Aug. 7 letter brushing off a request for a meeting with the American-Arab Anti-Discrimination Committee.

Contrast the current CBS response with the network's past reactions when network staffers made objectionable comments "in their personal capacity":

- Two years ago, "60 Minutes" commentator-lite Andy Rooney made derogatory remarks about blacks and gays to a journalist. "CBS News cannot tolerate such remarks or anything that approximates such comments since they in no way reflect the views of this organization," declared Ober's predecessor as president of CBS News, David Burke. Rooney was suspended for three months.

- When CBS sports analyst Jimmy "the Greek" Snyder made comments in a 1988 interview disparaging black athletes, CBS fired him. A top network official told the media: "CBS wishes to categorically disassociate itself from these remarks."

But in 1992, when it comes to anti-Arab comments, CBS is in no hurry to disassociate itself from anything.

Given the apparent double standard in CBS's responses, no wonder Arab-American groups are angry, and have been picketing CBS News headquarters in New York and Washington. They want apologies from Rather, CBS board member Kissinger and CBS analyst Ajami. They also want assurances that Rather and Ajami's personal tilt toward Israel won't result in biased coverage.

These activists do not accept Kissinger's explanation that his sweeping remark about Arab dishonesty was meant to refer only to Arab government officials.

Every so often, prejudice in powerful places comes to the surface in a way that dramatizes a chronic condition. That chronic condition remains: the acceptance of anti-Arab bigotry in mainstream media.

When bias is tolerated at a news outlet, responsibility usually rests at the top. CBS board chair Laurence Tisch is known to be a staunch Israel supporter who bristles on the rare occasions when CBS News exposes Israeli government duplicity.

If a CBS associate had made, or tolerated, an anti-Semitic comment like "You can't really believe anything an Israeli says," one suspects that individual's career at CBS might have been over.

But in this case, when the aggrieved people were Arabs, CBS took only evasive action.

August 12, 1992

It Took an Explosion
to Wake Up News Media

It was an amazing discovery for network TV and other national news media. Within hours of the Simi Valley jury's acquittals in the beating of Rodney King, they unearthed millions of people living in America's desperate inner cities.

What followed were rare TV specials and magazine cover stories about urban poverty and neglect. Ted Koppel even hosted a "Nightline In South Central."

If many Americans had been stunned by the Los Angeles riots, none were caught more off-guard than national news outlets.

That America's poor urban areas are powder kegs ready to explode had been highlighted in other mediums. You could hear it in rap music, or see it in such movies as "Do The Right Thing" and "Boyz N The Hood."

But in most national news media, this reality was no big deal—despite being in the middle of an election campaign, when our most pressing problems are supposed to receive a full airing.

Until L.A. erupted, the inner city was a non-issue in campaign '92. Political journalists regularly dismissed blacks as just another selfish "special interest" group—sort of like the natural gas lobby.

Media pundits openly instructed candidates to ignore the concerns of blacks, Latinos and the poor, and appeal instead to "the middle class"—a codephrase that began to sound like "just us white folks."

Cutting against the orthodoxy of the pundits, Jesse Jackson kept trying—with little success—to get presidential candidates like Bill Clinton to forthrightly discuss "the urban agenda." Jackson's efforts earned him the scorn of national media.

Days before the Rodney King riots, a supposedly objective *New York Times* news article began: "Jesse Jackson, who has twice run for President and knows a thing or two about creating mischief within the Democratic party, avoided endorsing Governor Bill Clinton today…"

When calling upon the Democrats to stand for racial justice is portrayed as "creating mischief"—and constituencies such as blacks and Latinos (20 percent of the country) are dismissed as "special interests"—media bias is quite pronounced.

In fact, since 1990, many news outlets have seemed less concerned about racism than about the allegedly overzealous activists who challenge inequality—denounced as "politically correct" in countless media stories.

A computer search of the term "politically correct"—conducted by FAIR analyst Steve Rendall—found that the *Los Angeles Times* published 252 articles containing this putdown in the last six months alone. The media obsession with disparaging activists helped obscure the fact that racial bigotry and hate crimes have been on the rise.

A National Opinion Research Center poll in 1990 showed widespread prejudice against every racial minority group, especially blacks: 53 percent of non-black respondents thought African-Americans were less intelligent than whites; 56 percent believed them to be more violence-prone; and 78 percent said they were more likely to "prefer to live off welfare" than to be self-supporting.

This poll offers clues to the racial attitudes that the 12 jurors took with them into the Simi Valley jury room.

Far from raising consciousness about racism, news media have often reinforced stereotypes. Little has changed since a 1987 *Columbia Journalism Review* study conducted by researcher Kirk Johnson found that mainstream media coverage of two black neighborhoods in Boston focused overwhelmingly on stories involving crime, violence and drugs: "85 percent reinforced negative stereotypes of blacks."

By contrast, Boston's African-American media during the same period provided a more multifaceted story, which—while not ignoring crime—revealed "a black community thirsty for educational advancement and entrepreneurial achievement, and eager to remedy poor living conditions made worse by bureaucratic neglect."

Of course, occasional mainstream news reports deserve credit for exposing racism. In September 1991, for example, a segment on ABC's "Primetime Live" offered powerful proof that racial discrimination is far from a thing of the past. The program dispatched two well-dressed, university-educated types—one black, one white—to apply for jobs with the same employer, to rent apartments from the same landlord, and to buy a used car from the same dealer. ABC's hidden cameras recorded that again and again, the black man was lied to or cheated.

When it comes to issues of race, national journalists—especially those based in the black-majority city of Washington—need to get out of the clubby atmosphere of officialdom and think tanks, and into the streets.

There they might run into 80-year-old Studs Terkel, one of the few journalists not caught off-guard by events in Los Angeles. Working independently with his ears at street level, Terkel wrote his prophetic new book—*Race: How Blacks and Whites Think and Feel About the American Obsession*—well before the first match was lit.

May 6, 1992

Institutional Racism in Media: The Verdict Is In

No one knows what the verdict will be for the four Los Angeles police officers now on trial in federal court for violating Rodney King's civil rights when they beat him. The jury's decision is being anxiously awaited around the country.

But another verdict due soon also has major implications for social justice in the United States. The nation's press is in the dock. The charge: institutional racism.

Every spring the American Society of Newspaper Editors releases the results of its annual survey on "minority professionals in the newsroom." And every time, the new statistics confirm an old story. Progress is slow. Very slow.

If the nation's top editors were as committed to fiscal solvency as they've been to racial balance, hundreds of daily papers publishing today would have gone bankrupt long ago.

Back in 1978—when its figures showed minority staffers at 4 percent—the editors' organization set a goal of "achieving minority employment at daily newspapers that matches minority representation in the general U.S. population by the year 2000, or sooner." In 1992 the total reached 9.4 percent. At that rate the parity goal won't be met until around 2020.

On the recent 25th anniversary of the Kerner Commission Report about the causes of urban riots, various news outlets bluntly stated that little has changed since the 1968 presidential panel documented extreme racial inequities.

But these media retrospectives ignored a key aspect of the Kerner Report—a call for reform of the news industry itself. Many of the biggest U.S. news operations were virtually all-white in 1968. The Kerner Report blasted "tokenism," in effect calling for newsrooms to look like America.

Today, African-Americans account for only 4.8 percent of the nation's daily newspaper journalists, while comprising 12.1 percent of the U.S. population according to the latest census.

The figures are much lower for employment of Hispanics (2.6 percent), Asian-Americans (1.7 percent) and Native Americans (0.3 percent)—all represented in newsrooms far below their presence in the country.

There are exceptions. Certain daily newspapers aggressively pursue staff diversity. Nationally, the Gannett and Knight-Ridder chains have taken the lead.

But 51 percent of dailies—mainly the smaller ones—still have entirely white newsrooms. They represent a third of daily U.S. circulation.

The Kerner Commission stressed the need for minorities in decision-making positions: "Newspaper and television policies are, generally speaking, not set by reporters. Editorial decisions about which stories to cover and which to use are made by editors. Yet, very few Negroes in this country are involved in making these decisions..."

Those words are chilling today. While lately the newspaper industry is hiring minority journalists for entry-level jobs at a rate on a par with the U.S. population, the power remains firmly in white hands. Caucasians hold 93.7 percent of the supervisory newsroom jobs. And well above the glass ceiling, the ranks of publishers and owners are almost as lily-white as in the Jim Crow era.

As Barbara Reynolds, an outspoken editor at *USA Today*, puts it: "The vast majority of editorial writers and news managers live in the suburbs and have long since stopped caring about the cities. To them, the homeless, poor health care and street crime have lost their urgency."

News magazines, which are less open about minority staff data than newspapers, apparently have a worse employment record. And the situation is little better in radio and television.

Public TV has been a keen disappointment. Aside

from "Tony Brown's Journal" (with its Republican host promoting entrepreneurial approaches for blacks), PBS has failed to support ongoing national programs with black people retaining creative control. A case in point: "Street Life," an independent TV news magazine produced by Chicago-based journalist Delmarie Cobb.

The first two "Street Life" programs aired on public TV stations in 50 markets across the country. But despite the quality of the hour-long shows, PBS has refused to provide any funding. Cobb says she's gotten feedback from PBS headquarters that the show is "too black."

At a PBS conference unveiling national programs for the current season, Cobb found, "Almost every program...was a celebration of white ancestry, history or genius. It is as if people of color have made no significant contributions to the world."

A letter from a PBS vice president to Cobb conceded that "there were more animals on our preview reel than people of color but the preview reel was featuring four new series—'The Kennedys,' 'The Space Age,' 'Realms of the Russian Bear' and 'Dinosaurs.'"

Every once in a while—as when Los Angeles was burning last spring—mainstream media rush into some introspection about racism. But after the hot news has cooled, it's media business as usual again.

March 17, 1993

Gay Rights and News "Balance"

Houston

Many top Republicans are determined to make homosexuality a winning issue for George Bush in the fall campaign. And they're hoping the news media will help out.

Republican strategists are gambling that little has changed in media attitudes since *Parade* magazine fondly reminisced in a 1987 article: "The '50s, viewed through the rosy prism of nostalgia, were the good old days.... Homosexuals stayed in the closet, not on the front pages."

Gay men and lesbians, speaking out for equal rights, are no longer strangers to the front pages. But anti-gay prejudices run deep in U.S. society, and Bush's managers seem eager to fuel a backlash against gays in the closing months of the '92 campaign.

Before the Republican convention, senior Bush-Quayle adviser Charles Black condemned Bill Clinton for having "adopted the gay agenda." At the convention, gay baiting was almost as incessant as oil drilling used to be around Houston. Signs proclaimed: "Family Rights Forever/'Gay' Rights Never!"

In response to the onslaught, GOP fundraiser Marvin Liebman—who is gay—commented: "We [gays] have replaced the communists as the No. 1 menace to all that they pronounce is good and traditional in American life." Observed Robert Bray of the National Gay and Lesbian Task Force: "We're the Willie Hortons of 1992."

The anti-gay backlash is gaining momentum this election year.

In Oregon, a well-financed fundamentalist coalition allied with Rev. Pat Robertson has placed a measure on the November ballot that would amend the state constitution to declare homosexuality an abnormality. The measure would prohibit human rights guarantees for gays and require pub-

lic schools to teach that gay people are "abnormal, wrong, unnatural and perverse." [The initiative lost at the polls.]

Colorado voters will decide on a constitutional amendment this November that would prohibit gay rights laws in that state. [The amendment passed.]

When covering anti-gay crusades, mainstream journalists have assumed their traditional posture of "balance"—not acknowledging that gay rights are human rights. In practice, "neutrality" often means reinforcing prejudice, as it did years ago in coverage of the struggle against racism.

During the 1950s and early '60s, there was nothing noble or professional about journalists who continued to provide equal space and stature to civil rights leaders and bigots alike. Advocacy of racial segregation and discrimination was treated then as a legitimate point-of-view—not bigotry.

In November 1960, for example, network TV showcased a pro-and-con debate on segregation between Martin Luther King Jr. and James J. Kilpatrick. Then a Richmond newspaper editor, Kilpatrick offered high-toned language in defense of the racial status quo. It's not that he disliked black people, argued Kilpatrick, but he worried that integration would erase "every distinction of race" in society.

Like the old debates on racial segregation, today's media discussions about gays typically feature bigots— usually religious fundamentalists—offering lofty verbiage to justify hatred and discrimination. The fundamentalists "don't hate homosexuals," they assure us, but just believe gays should not have equal rights to jobs, benefits, housing. Equal rights, it's argued, would "sanction an abomination."

Vilifying certain people because of who and how they love would be far less acceptable to the public if mass media offered regular coverage puncturing the prejudices and fears that surround attitudes toward gays.

Three years ago the *San Francisco Examiner* broke through the stereotypes with a 16-day, 64-page "Gay in

America" series, offering a multidimensional look at a diverse spectrum of lesbians and gay men. Sadly, the depiction of people who are gay as people—no more or less human than the rest of humanity—is still a revelation for many Americans.

The Bush-Quayle campaign seems bent on pandering to those who oppose human rights for gay people. Journalists may fancy themselves as caught in the middle of a polarized debate. But human rights and independent journalism must reinforce each other. Or we will have neither.

August 19, 1992

Part VII

Television: The More You Watch, the Less You Know

Most Americans get most of their news from TV. No wonder so many myths prevail. Conventional wisdoms, simplistic soundbites and sudden calamities dominate the television screen; insights about social realities are few and far between.

TOM TOMORROW©

What Voters Don't Know May Hurt Them

"What did he know, and when did he know it?" That's become the standard question to ask about presidents brushed with scandal.

But results of an October 1992 poll suggest that we should be asking a different question: "What does the average voter know, and why does he or she know so little?"

Don't get us wrong. We aren't primarily blaming the public. In fact, the survey of public knowledge about the presidential candidates and issues points toward other culprits—television and the news media overall.

The nationwide telephone poll of 600 likely voters found them to be inundated by media. Most said television is their main source of information, while the majority reported watching a TV news program virtually every day. Most also said they regularly read a newspaper.

It's not that the public is totally uninformed. "Selectively misinformed" would be more accurate. The more trivial the information, the better the media seem to be at communicating it.

For example, 86 percent of the voting public knows that the Bush family has a dog named Millie, and 89 percent could identify Murphy Brown as the TV character criticized by Vice President Dan Quayle.

In sharp contrast, only 19 percent could identify the Reagan cabinet member recently indicted in the Iran-Contra scandal: Caspar Weinberger.

Even on an issue that intensified the week the poll was conducted—with George Bush vetoing legislation to enact sanctions against China because of human rights abuses—much of the voting public is "out of the loop." Almost as many people believe Bush imposed sanctions on China as know his actual position: retaining China's "most favored nation" status.

The new survey—which was commissioned by FAIR, the media watch group with which we are associated—went beyond typical mass media polls. Besides asking voters for their opinions, it also probed to find out what information, if any, shaped those opinions.

The answers are hardly encouraging to those who hope for an informed electorate.

A media strategist for George Bush, however, might take solace that—despite Bush's standing in popularity polls—some of his most ferocious, and distorted, attacks are getting through to voters.

On the "tax and spend" theme, voters hold many misconceptions that favor the Bush campaign. Thirty-two percent answered that Arkansas state taxes are "among the highest in the nation," compared to only 21 percent who responded *correctly* that taxes in Governor Bill Clinton's home state are among the lowest.

As to whether Congress spent more or less money last year than requested by President Bush in his budget, only 22 percent answered *correctly* that Bush's budget called for more than Congress actually spent. Three times as many people (66 percent) answered inaccurately that Congress was the bigger spender. Blame national news media for ignorance of this fact.

Professors Justin Lewis and Michael Morgan, who supervised the poll in collaboration with the University of Massachusetts Center for the Study of Communication, say their findings rebut claims of a "liberal media" biased against the GOP.

"Many voters have absorbed deceptive Republican attacks against Clinton," Lewis and Morgan conclude. "It's due in part to news media emphasis on reporting campaign rhetoric rather than the facts, and their reluctance to focus on the record rather than on 'claims' about the record."

The survey reveals deep ignorance among voters on basic subjects, such as how the federal government spends

Election '92 - Final Exam

1.) Which of the following political figures could not be identified by most T.V. viewers?

A.)Best selling White House dog.

B.)Unwed T.V. sitcom character.

C.) Indicted former Sec. of Defense.

their tax money. Asked whether more money goes to "foreign aid" or "the military" or "welfare," 42 percent selected foreign aid, which accounts for only 1 percent of spending. Almost a third of the respondents chose welfare, which is just 5 percent of the federal budget.

The correct answer is military spending—more than four times larger than federal welfare spending. It was chosen by a mere 22 percent of those responding.

Heavy TV news viewers were the most uninformed about federal spending, as were Bush and Perot supporters. Professors Lewis and Morgan attribute the misconceptions to intensive coverage of the "welfare problem" and foreign aid, and to reporting on military spending that emphasizes cutbacks and job losses.

Whatever the particular explanations for the various incorrect answers, the survey as a whole indicates that the problem is more serious than simple ignorance.

As columnist Walter Lippmann once wrote, "Misleading news is worse than none at all." In 1992, thanks in part to mass media, much of what Americans "know" just isn't so.

October 14, 1992

Local TV News Ethic: "If It Bleeds, It Leads"

Step off a plane anywhere in the United States, tune into the local TV news programs, and you're likely to see a succession of reports on murders, shootouts, rapes, traffic wrecks, fires and other grisly events.

In many local TV newsrooms, the tacit rule is: "If it bleeds, it leads." Often, the more lurid the story the better its chances of topping the broadcast. The results are a lot closer to "America's Most Wanted" or "A Current Affair" than anything that might make a journalist feel proud.

Spinning the dial is unlikely to provide relief. The same stories, reported in much the same way, can be found on different channels.

When writer Carol Tice taped and analyzed a week of evening news broadcasts from seven local TV stations in Los Angeles, her 1990 report in the weekly *L.A. Reader* could have been titled "How I Survived My Week in Hell."

As the week began, the top "local" TV news story was mass murder by a mad gunman about 2,700 miles away in Florida, with video close-ups of grieving relatives. Other big stories of the week included the kidnapping of two girls, black-and-white surveillance film of gang members robbing a convenience store, and plane crash pictures with dramatic audio from the cockpit.

Violent calamities—breathlessly narrated with arresting footage of police tape, body bags and the like—fascinate TV news programmers. But context is usually absent; attention is lavished on tragic events, but not on what might have caused (or prevented) them.

Intent on providing adrenalin-pumping visuals, local TV coverage is apt to emulate the bang-bang tone of prime-time dramas, augmented by comments from tearful loved ones, witnesses and police.

Dramatic crime reports and brief news items are accompanied by anchors' "happy talk" chatter, weather and sports reports...and, of course, plenty of commercials—about one minute of ads for every four minutes of "news." To round out the show, local broadcasts commonly close with a cuddly "human interest" story affirming the basic goodness of the community.

It all may be a bit bewildering, but TV news is not about making sense—it's about making money. Lots of it.

While layoffs and cost-cutting have been common in news departments, advertiser dollars are drawn to local TV news, partly because—as the *New York Times* has put it—"many sponsors think news programs attract affluent viewers." It's a winning combination for the owners, and a loser for the public.

Even when dealing with substantive topics, local TV news reporting tends to be shoddy. In 1990 the *Columbia Journalism Review* published a devastating account by a researcher who spent 50 days inside TV newsrooms in several metropolitan areas.

"Overall, 18 of the 32 stories analyzed—56 percent—were inaccurate or misleading," reported John McManus, director of the journalism program at Santa Clara University in California. Making matters worse, "often the station made no effort to correct obvious omissions."

McManus found a pattern to the mis-coverage: "There is an economic logic to these distortions and inaccuracies. All but one...were likely to increase the story's appeal, help cut down the cost of reporting, or oversimplify a story so it could be told in two minutes."

Some TV newsrooms trim budgets by using free footage provided by PR departments of various corporations and other well-financed institutions. Many times the hardly-impartial provider of these "video press releases" is not identified.

The Fox-TV affiliate in Los Angeles aired "four major PR stories" in a single night, according to Tice's research.

Stories showcased a Las Vegas hotel opening ("the same montage appeared on every station"); construction of the Richard Nixon library, with no mention of the words "Watergate" or "resigned"; and a press tour of Northrop's Stealth bomber factory—footage provided, unacknowledged, by the company.

A report on Starkist's introduction of dolphin-safe tuna featured "loving closeups of tuna cans" and mascot Charlie Tuna, but not the long consumer boycott that had pressured Starkist to change its fishing practices.

The abysmal condition of most local TV news largely reflects a deregulated broadcast industry that has scant commitment to the public interest, and fervent commitment to maximizing profits.

Eager to know what's going on in their neighborhoods and in the region, many people who have a low opinion of local TV news end up watching it anyway. What they see on television—night after night—ignores major issues, and hobbles the ability of communities to confront their problems.

February 3, 1993

TV's Harvest of Shame

When Americans tuned into CBS the night after Thanksgiving in 1960, they saw a gripping hour-long report about the nation's migrant farm workers—"Harvest of Shame."

Carefully crafted by a network news crew that followed migrant workers through the cycle of the seasons, "Harvest of Shame" stands a third of a century later as a two-count indictment—of agribusiness that still treats employees abysmally, and of a TV business that has largely forsaken hard-hitting journalism.

Today, network television avoids tough reporting that takes on injustice. Few of its news programs will be vividly remembered in 32 days…let alone 32 years.

At the outset of "Harvest of Shame," correspondent Edward R. Murrow quoted a farmer: "We used to own our slaves. Now we just rent them."

Murrow did not pose as equivocal or neutral. "These are the migrants—workers in the sweatshops of the soil," he intoned, introducing "the men, women and children who harvest the crops in this country of ours—the best-fed nation on Earth. These are the forgotten people: the underprotected, the undereducated, the underclothed, the underfed."

Farm workers spoke painfully of their hopes—for a home, square meals, education for their children. Prodded by a CBS interviewer, they acknowledged that those dreams were unlikely to be fulfilled. One man, standing with his family near a ditch where they'd spent the night, was asked how much money he had in the world. His reply: a dollar and 45 cents.

The black-and-white footage is more vivid than today's high-tech TV visuals because the producers clearly believed in the profound importance of each human being. The cameras lingered over the faces. The children are heart-breaking to watch.

In a migrant camp, while parents worked in the fields, viewers saw kids lucky enough to receive lunch: a half-pint of milk and a cracker.

Murrow's narration was focused like a tight beam of light. With the screen showing migrants packed into trucks for a long journey, Murrow bitingly observed that regulations for transport of produce and cattle were stronger than safeguards for farm laborers.

Later he contrasted the elaborate new stables for horses at a nearby racetrack with the squalid conditions at a migrant camp. And later, a honed edge in his voice, Murrow noted that federal appropriations were more devoted to the well-being of migratory wildlife than migratory children.

Unlike his blow-dried and high-paid successors, Murrow explicitly connected social injustice with the policies that caused it. At the close of "Harvest of Shame," Murrow put on his glasses to read recommendations from a commission on migrant workers—child labor laws, health and education programs, workers compensation, decent housing.

Then Murrow took off his glasses and looked sternly into the camera. At us. "There will of course," he said briskly, "be opposition to these recommendations—'too much government interference,' 'too expensive,' 'socialism.'"

Murrow appeared almost distraught, but resolute, as he continued: "The migrants have no lobby. Only an enlightened, aroused and perhaps angered public opinion can do anything about the migrants. The people you have seen have the strength to harvest your fruit and vegetables. They do not have the strength to influence legislation. Maybe we do. Good night and good luck."

Years later, the executive producer of "Harvest of Shame," Fred Friendly, commented that "corporations exercise a kind of positive veto" which determines TV programming. If no one wants to pay for a big project, it

doesn't happen. That's why this Thanksgiving weekend you won't be seeing anything like "Harvest of Shame" on a major TV network.

The problem extends to so-called public television. In 1990, PBS "Frontline" aired a 30-years-later update called "New Harvest, Old Shame," showing that many of the wretched conditions exposed by Murrow still remain. But such programs are rare. Much more common is the kind of special scheduled on public TV's "Nightly Business Report" for Thanksgiving Day 1992: "The NBR Guide to Stock Market Strategies."

Meanwhile, farm workers are almost invisible on TV. A Nexis computer search for the first 320 days of 1992 turned up only two stories on all-news CNN about the conditions facing farm workers. None were found on ABC News.

Yet there is plenty to report. The predominantly black and Latino farm labor force is still at risk. *People* magazine's special report 30 years after "Harvest of Shame" found that "migrants have a disability rate five times that of workers in any other industry—pesticide exposure alone affects 300,000 a year. And most get no paid holidays, sick days, overtime, retirement or disability plans or medical coverage." Wages sometimes amount to less than a dollar an hour.

Farm workers are so low on the media agenda that even a rare stand on their behalf by a Cabinet officer gets little notice. In July 1990, Labor Secretary Elizabeth Dole developed a plan to monitor conditions: "I have personally witnessed the deplorable living and working conditions of some migrant farm workers," said a Dole memo. "I was shocked and deeply moved."

Soon after key parts of her plan were stifled by the White House, Dole resigned her post; sources say the blunting of the migrant-worker plan figured in her decision. But to the news media, the episode was no big deal.

November 18, 1992

Part VIII

Campaign Horse-Racing

The making of the president 1992 was an exercise in protracted media warfare and manipulation. The press designated campaign frontrunners well before the first primary ballots were cast; disdained pretenders to the Oval Office throne were summarily dismissed. And as for issues—media frames kept many out of the picture.

"We Aren't Biased Against the Mad, Bomb-Throwing, Yuppie Monk"

When Pennsylvania primary voters confirmed that Jerry Brown was out of the running for the White House in late April 1992, it was a big victory for Bill Clinton—and for a national press corps that opposed the former California governor with equal vigor.

Like any politician, Brown deserves tough coverage. But no presidential candidate in recent memory has been more tarred and feathered with media putdowns and epithets than Jerry Brown.

In *Newsweek* he was described as "the mad monk of presidential politics," a "masterful annoyance" and "the Zen Yuppie." *Time* magazine called him "a walking Experiment in Living" with "terminal flightiness."

Those were the polite descriptions.

Most journalists expressed irritation: CNN's Bernard Shaw referred to him as "a pain in the you-know-what." ABC's Ted Koppel called him "annoying."

Other labels were so loaded they implied imminent violence. NBC's Lisa Myers called him "the political equivalent of a drive-by shooting." David Gergen on Mac-Neil/Lehrer termed him a "political assassin."

"Governor Moonbeam" was not pejorative enough for *Newsweek*, which renamed Brown "Governor Panderbeam" because of his efforts to attract the votes of Michigan's union members. Many politicians have courted the support of both environmentalists and labor. When Brown did it, *Time* dubbed him "Samuel Gompers in Earth shoes" and a "noisy sideshow for dyspeptic interest groups."

Selling oneself to the voters is what all candidates do. When Brown did it, he was "as brash as a late night television pitchman" or "an odd, fringe actor shouting an 800 telephone number."

Ask journalists about their steady stream of ridicule aimed at Brown, and they go into denial: Us? Biased? Impossible!

After Brown's victory in the Connecticut primary in March, the *New York Times* interviewed TV network executives about Brown's charge that the "establishment media" had consistently ignored or belittled his campaign. No way, they responded.

"He's still in the race," said ABC's spokesperson. "It can't have affected him too much." In other words, since media mistreatment hadn't driven Brown out of the race, no problem.

In fact, the bias was apparent from day one. During the first nationally-televised presidential debate, NBC anchor Tom Brokaw tried to prevent Brown from making a fundraising appeal. Brown defended his right to ask for small donations since "General Electric, which owns NBC, gave $350,000 to incumbents last year."

The next day, all four pundits on CNN's "Crossfire" show—which is sponsored by GE—laughed at Brown as if he were the country's newest national joke; "Crossfire" refused to put Brown on the air when he insisted on his right to give out his 800 number.

Months later, on the day Brown defeated Clinton in Connecticut, he was still being dismissed as a nuisance in a *New York Times* report, which described him as "flailing about, spewing out charges like sparks from a Fourth of July pinwheel, in a last-ditch effort to establish himself…as a credible alternative."

On the eve of the New York primary, a *Newsweek* article on the *positive* aspects of Brown's campaign referred to him as "a chameleon, a character assassin and a first-class cynic." (Faint praise indeed.) It accused the candidate of "engaging in his typical hype" and his supporters of "turning a blind eye to their candidate's unfitness."

Reporting about Brown has been so derisive for so many months, it's difficult to remember that journalists rarely refer to candidates that way. Can anyone imagine a *Newsweek* senior editor writing matter-of-factly about George Bush's "typical hype" or his "unfitness"?

Mainstream news hounds, many of whom hardly noticed big tax giveaways to the rich a decade ago, became growling bulldogs on the scent of Brown's dubious flat tax plan. If President Reagan's regressive tax proposals had received the same kind of media hounding, the tax tables Americans consulted this year would have been a lot fairer.

Reporters have—quite correctly—highlighted the fact that the same Jerry Brown who now runs against big money politics was a short while ago part of that corrupt system. For this, he was dubbed a "hypocrite." Politicians still dependent on big donors are praised as "viable."

Given the uneven playing field resulting from Brown's refusal to cater to monied interests while Bill Clinton (and George Bush) raise and spend millions of dollars from the wealthy, it's striking that national media fail to report on which candidate has won more "votes per dollar spent" this year.

This "VPDS" count would be quite informative to voters and might put Brown's campaign in clearer focus. If media outlets did such reporting, self-critical stories would probably follow as journalists pondered whether they were "too sympathetic to Brown."

Jerry Brown got as far as he did in 1992 despite a national press corps bent on belittling him. If Brown decides to make a run for the Presidency again, he'll have to figure out how to overcome not only big money politics, but big media as well.

April 29, 1992

The Convention's Coming:
It's Jackson-Bashing Season

It's become a media ritual: Every four years, as the Democratic National Convention approaches, the bashing goes into high gear.

Time magazine grouped him among "whiners" and "megalomaniacs." CNN analyst Frederick Allen asserted that many Democrats "would love to see" him "exposed as a straw man, and he may be setting himself on fire." *Newsweek*'s conventional wisdom labeled him an "egotistical party wrecker."

On the eve of another Democratic convention, the political press corps is in a familiar battle formation—laying siege against Jesse Jackson. His media image in recent weeks has been only slightly better than John Gotti's.

The latest round of denunciations was triggered by Bill Clinton's speech to a conference of Jackson's Rainbow Coalition. In that speech, the governor criticized a little-known black rapper, Sister Souljah, for her provocative comments about whites made to a reporter a month earlier. (Souljah appeared briefly at the Rainbow conference.)

Commentators and political reporters were nearly unanimous in applauding Clinton's "courage" in standing up to bigotry. Lost in much of the praise was the fact that Clinton's attack on Souljah was a calculated effort to offend Jackson and his supporters—less a bold stand on principle than a political gambit.

The *Washington Post* foreshadowed it as such the day *before* the speech: "Some top advisers to Clinton argue that...he must become involved in highly publicized confrontations with one or more Democratic constituencies." Key aides wanted him to "confront [Jackson] and his followers."

Rainbow Coalition members who'd hoped Clinton

would use his speech to spotlight serious proposals for urban America, working people or family farmers were stunned when he chose instead to divert attention to a militant rap singer.

But the media pundits were thrilled. Attacking Murphy Brown may have been silly; denouncing a black rapper was bold.

If African-American activists were used as props for Clinton's premeditated "highly publicized confrontation," the prize was supposed to be white voters—the so-called "Reagan Democrats"—presumed to be horrified by the specter of racial equality.

The truth is that Clinton's Souljah gambit had similarities to George Bush's Willie Horton commercial of 1988. Both were aimed at winning white votes by focusing attention on a diversion that stoked fears of black violence. The *New York Times* vehemently denied the link, headlining its editorial: "Sister Souljah Is No Willie Horton." That day's news report in the *Times* carried the pseudo-objective headline: "Clinton Deftly Navigates Shoals of Racial Issues."

Besides being courageous and moral, the pundits told us, Clinton's speech at the Rainbow event was brilliant strategy. CNN's Jack Germond, one of TV's "liberals," enthused that Clinton was "doing some very smart politics; I think he's doing some dynamite politics, in fact."

Some political writers argue that Clinton did so well with black voters in the primaries, he doesn't need Jackson's support. These "experts" fail to point out that few blacks felt involved enough to vote in the primaries, and that a low black turnout in November spells defeat for Clinton.

Despite the accolades for Clinton, the goal of the pundits was not so much to praise Clinton...as to bury Jackson. They try it every four years.

With Jackson the villain in this quadrennial melodrama, Democratic presidential nominees take turns being the news media's great white hope to put him in his place.

Walter Mondale was judged insufficiently firm in '84. Four years later, media savants egged on Michael Dukakis to "stand up to" Jackson, who'd finished a strong second for the nomination. Dukakis obliged at the Atlanta convention, eager to show he wouldn't "cave in" to groups the media denigrate as "special interests"—blacks, labor, poor people, seniors.

Today's coverage is a rerun—with Jackson causing "mischief" or "agony" or "trouble" for the Democrats. CNN's Germond recently declared: "The one thing that any Democratic candidate has to worry about is being seen as a prisoner of constituencies, and the constituencies include organized labor and they obviously include black voters who vote overwhelmingly for the Democratic Party."

Party leaders keep listening to sages who proclaim that turning off loyal constituencies is the way to win elections. If one day a Democratic presidential nominee quits listening to the pundits, something unusual might happen: an electoral victory. [In retrospect, Clinton managed to run a winning campaign while alternately heeding and confounding the pundits.]

July 1, 1992

Republicans Work the Media Refs

With so many Republicans moonlighting as media critics these days, expect to hear a lot about journalistic bias against George Bush and Dan Quayle between now and November.

Senator Mitch McConnell complains about "the Democrats and their friends in the media...firing their guns at George Bush." Even Barbara Bush has pushed the blame-the-media spin, lecturing Judy Woodruff about alleged bias during a recent interview on PBS.

When Republican Senate Whip Alan Simpson declared at his party's convention that Americans are "fed up with the media," it wasn't the first time he'd assumed the role of press critic. Before Iraq invaded Kuwait two years ago, Simpson privately assured Saddam Hussein that his image problem in the U.S. was not with the government, but with America's "haughty and pampered press." Even Saddam was a victim of the liberal media.

During the convention at the Astrodome, Republican Party chair Rich Bond was so affronted by one *Houston Chronicle* headline—"Quayle Tries to Play Up Martyr Role"—that he kept displaying it to journalists as evidence of media bias.

But in a moment of candor, Bond provided insight into the Republicans' media-bashing: "There is some strategy to it," he told the *Washington Post*. "I'm the coach of kids' basketball and Little League teams. If you watch any great coach, what they try to do is 'work the refs.' Maybe the ref will cut you a little slack next time."

Intent on blaming others for their ticket's low standing in the polls, Bush-Quayle strategists are targeting national news media as handy scapegoats.

Never mind that these same media acted as cheerlead-

ers for President Bush's deadly invasion of Panama—pumping his approval ratings through the roof.

Never mind that Bush's popularity soared even higher after these news outlets fawned over him during the Gulf War, serving more as a fourth branch of government than the fourth estate.

In politics, nothing succeeds like success—or fails like failure. When George Bush was riding high, mainstream news media boosted him even higher. The president's backers were pleased to ride the waves of biased pro-Bush coverage for years. But, as Bush sank in the polls along with leading economic indicators, the media's genuflecting finally gave way to some blunt coverage.

The GOP gathering in Houston was supposed to turn things around. But Bush handlers didn't like some of the convention coverage because it accurately depicted a national Republican Party that has lurched to the right—with Bush caving in to religious fundamentalists.

A platform that outlaws abortions even in cases of rape or incest might reasonably be called "extreme," but such descriptions raise the hackles of Republican functionaries.

Despite the complaints, U.S. media coverage of the Republican Convention was, if anything, understated—especially when compared to what foreign media reported. A news account in one conservative British daily referred to Republican delegates as "the stormtroopers for Family Values."

On American TV, Patrick Buchanan's declaration of "cultural war" earned bad marks from some pundits. But TV's savants mostly went dumb instead of pointing out that President Bush's acceptance speech was riddled with major distortions of fact—such as Clinton's phantom "128 tax hikes" in Arkansas or his nonexistent "plan for a massive government takeover of health care."

After Bush's speech, TV analysts seemed much more concerned with discussing the colorful balloon drop.

Network TV continued to apply the pejorative "special interests" label unevenly. At the Democratic Convention in New York, non-wealthy constituencies such as union members, African-Americans, environmentalists and gays were repeatedly portrayed as powerful and pesky "special interests."

In Houston, the big-money interests behind the Republican Party were not tagged with the "special interests" label. *Fortune* magazine has just reported that 85 percent of corporate CEOs want Bush reelected. But on national TV, big businesses are not referred to as "special interests"— presumably, they represent the "national interest."

Republican media watchdogs will keep growling about media unfairness to the Bush-Quayle campaign. As party chair Rich Bond admitted, yelling at the media from the sidelines is a tactic of "working the refs" in hopes they'll cut the GOP ticket "a little slack."

Journalists would do well to remember Bond's metaphor the next time they receive an angry call about bias from Bush-Quayle headquarters, or a stack of computer-generated postcards decrying "the liberal media."

August 26, 1992

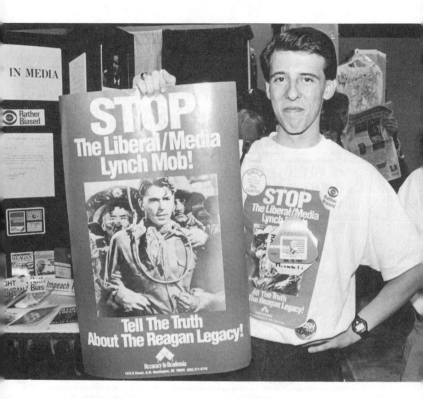

What Makes Big News?
—A Tale of Two Stories

With national media obsessing about Bill Clinton's draft history, the Democratic nominee has begun to moonlight as a media critic.

Clinton is denouncing a media "feeding frenzy about something that, even if it's true, doesn't amount to a hill of beans." The media should be focusing, says press critic Clinton, on new Iran-Contra evidence implicating George Bush—which, "if true, should call into question not only the president's veracity, but his support for illegal conduct."

When Clinton says that a small story (his draft record) is getting big media play, while a big story (Bush and Iran-Contra) is getting small play, he is doing what serious press critics do—sniffing out media double-standards.

Since Clinton is not exactly a disinterested party, let's scrutinize his charge of media bias.

The two stories are identical in one respect: Both candidates seem to be lying. Almost anyone who objectively studies the record will conclude that neither Bush on Iran-Contra, nor Clinton on how he evaded military induction, has been telling the truth.

Yet one story, Bush's Iran-Contra involvement, has had little visibility in campaign coverage this year. The new evidence against Bush is a 1987 memo dictated by Secretary of State George Shultz after a phone conversation with Defense Secretary Caspar "Cap" Weinberger. The memo states: "V.P. [Bush] in papers yesterday said he [was] not exposed to Cap or my arguments on Iran arms. Cap called me and said that's terrible. He [Bush] was on the other side. It's on the record. Why did he say that?"

The memo adds still another piece of evidence that Bush is not telling the truth when he claims—as he has for five years—that he was "not in the loop" about arms sales to

Iran, and was unaware that Shultz and Weinberger strongly opposed the sales.

But it's the other story, Clinton's evasions about his draft evasion, that have received massive coverage lately. Viewers of CNN, for example, saw it hashed and rehashed as a news item on Sept. 15, and again that night in a full hour of "Larry King Live" and a 30-minute "Crossfire" debate. (On "Crossfire," Clinton's ethics and honesty were savaged by Oliver North, whose shredding of Iran-Contra documents may have saved Bush's career.) That night's "MacNeil/Lehrer NewsHour" on PBS and "Nightline" on ABC also focused on Clinton and the draft.

Which story is more newsworthy? This is the nub of the issue, and breaks down into several key points.

- Timeliness: Iran-Contra is far more recent, having occurred six or seven years ago. Bill Clinton's draft maneuvering is relatively ancient, having occurred 23 years ago.

- Public vs. Private: Whatever Bill Clinton did in 1969, he did as a private citizen. In 1985-86, George Bush held the second highest office in the land.

- Weightiness: Like many other young men in the 1960s, Bill Clinton pulled strings and used contacts to avoid Vietnam, a war he opposed. Clinton did not write the draft laws, nor did he break them. The laws, fashioned by a Congress that included George Bush, allowed upper-middle-class and better-connected youths to avoid or delay induction, through deferments for graduate school and the like.

If Clinton had been a gung-ho believer in the war, but wanted others to fight it, that would be a more solid news story. A number of such politicians now serve in the U.S. Senate and the president's cabinet.

The fact is that Bill Clinton's actions to avoid Vietnam would barely be newsworthy had he come clean from the beginning.

By contrast, there is nothing trivial about Bush's role in the Iran-Contra affair. The evidence is overwhelming that his vice presidential office was fully aware of the illegal effort to arm the Nicaraguan Contra guerrillas—after Congress had prohibited it. Secretly subverting the law should be a major issue for any president or would-be president. And by all available evidence—including the new memo— Bush also knew about, and supported, the sale of weapons to the Iranian regime.

Media under-coverage of Bush's role in the biggest White House scandal since Watergate reflects a double standard: national news outlets continually invoke the "trust" issue about Clinton, but not about Bush.

When Bill Clinton talks about his draft history and George Bush talks about his far more important Iran-Contra record, they both keep dissembling. But as the presidential race heads into its final weeks, only one of the candidates has had to pay for his untruths with persistent media hounding.

September 16, 1992

Debates: Beware of Unidentified Flying Buzzwords

Making sense out of presidential debates is no easy matter. But it can be done—if you watch out for unidentified flying buzzwords.

First, some reminders: Candidates strive to be ambiguous while sounding forthright. They try to depict their expedient choices as acts of courage. Meanwhile, opponents who do the same are accused of cowardly pandering.

No TelePrompTers are allowed during debates—but as candidates stare earnestly into the camera, invisible Tele-PrompTers will be whirring in their heads. The hope is to make memorized speeches and one-liners sound impromptu.

In a debate, more than in any other campaign activity, the political weaponry comes down to words. Candidates select only the loaded ones.

It's true that the wrong cliche, ill-chosen and poorly aimed, can shoot a candidate in the foot. But the right one will find its mark: the voter.

As one of us wrote in a new book about politicians' rhetoric (*The Power of Babble* by Norman Solomon), "The best buzzwords commonly precede, and preempt, thought. Used correctly, they can guard against meaning—the most dangerous hazard of political language. Meaning causes big problems. And it's so unnecessary!"

Many of the foggy words spotlighted in the book are likely to be repeated during the debates, such as:

Middle Class

This is a purposely undefined category. A candidate wants to convey special concern for virtually all Americans, whether they make $20,000 in a good year or $100,000 in a bad one.

Sacrifice

Ten years—and many looted S&Ls and tax breaks for the wealthy—ago, President Reagan called for "sacrifices by the American people." The real question is: Who's being sacrificed, and who benefits? When Ross Perot or any other multimillionaire says we all have to sacrifice equally, it's time to get nervous.

Responsibility

It's a new rhetorical day for Democrats, signaled by Bill Clinton's oft-repeated calls for "responsible behavior" from "the people who benefit from government programs." That category could include polluting and price-gouging CEOs, but don't bet on it. Such lectures about responsibility are rarely aimed at the wealthy beneficiaries of government policies.

Empower

This one is rising on the jargon hit parade. A politician can mix messages nicely by proclaiming a commitment to "empower" people while conveying that they should depend on someone in power to empower them.

Big Government

This pejorative is customarily selective—referring only to government agencies that regulate corporate activities, or programs aiding poor and moderate-income people. It is rarely applied to military institutions with bloated budgets.

Tax and Spend

These are inevitable fiscal activities of a government, long made to sound diabolical by Republicans. When the 1992 Democratic Party platform declares a rejection of "the

big government theory that says we can hamstring business and tax and spend our way to prosperity," it is tromping onto some hallowed Republican ground.

On an upbeat note, the debates are likely to provide plenty of verbiage about "the family." Also expect "free enterprise" and "the private sector" to be regularly lauded.

On the other hand, "welfare" is a downer, to be mentioned only with a mixture of scorn and distaste. Many people approve of the social programs lumped together as "welfare" but don't like the word; the more politicians support such funding the less they refer to it that way, and vice versa.

Whatever you do, don't count on media pundits to decide who "won" each debate. Their subjective judgments are no better than yours—and in some cases their masks of ponderous objectivity hide strong biases.

Take George Will, for example. Will recently reminisced on ABC's "This Week With David Brinkley" about the 1980 debating duel between incumbent Jimmy Carter and presidential hopeful Ronald Reagan. What Will didn't mention—and what none of his colleagues in the studio were impolite enough to bring up—was the devious role he played in that historic event.

Back in 1980, George Will coached Reagan for his debate with Carter—and then had the audacity to praise Reagan's performance while analyzing the debate for ABC News, without mentioning his association with the Reagan campaign team!

Will prepped Reagan with the help of briefing materials stolen from the Carter White House. When these facts came to light years later, other journalists let George off with a polite scolding.

Expect George Will and his colleagues to rigorously evaluate the '92 debaters for honesty and integrity.

October 7, 1992

Media Blind Spots
on the Campaign Trail

The road to the White House was littered with media cliches in 1992. But some words and phrases were scrupulously avoided by mainstream journalists.

Anti-trust

Big media provided scant ink or air time for the view that corporations have grown too large and powerful. After Jerry Brown made Tom Brokaw sweat on an NBC-televised debate early in the campaign by slamming the network's owner General Electric, the candidate was depicted as a ridiculous pitchman with an 800 number.

By contrast, Paul Tsongas was a media darling who mentioned "anti-trust" only in the context of legal "constraints" that should be relaxed. Mega-media outlets seem uninterested in asking politicians where they stand on monopolization, a process that hurts consumers and workers. Is it any coincidence that so many cities have only one local daily newspaper, while a few news corporations are carving out large chunks of the media pie for themselves?

Poverty

Although news media frequently call for a "war on drugs," there is no such enthusiasm for an official battle against poverty.

It's true that "major" (media-anointed) candidates haven't done much to focus on poverty. But media failure to raise this issue lets candidates off the hook. And 1992 election reportage endorsed the notion that poor people don't merit the same rhetorical attention lavished on "the middle class."

A welcome exception came Oct. 27 with a CBS evening news report that offered insights about the "hard-working poor." Correspondent Bruce Morton ventured below the official poverty line—out of the usual bounds of the campaign trail.

Racism

Except for sensational mid-spring coverage of the Los Angeles riots and some thoughtful retrospectives later in the year, most news media relegated issues of racial discrimination and unequal opportunity to a back burner. Like the raisin in the sun described by Langston Hughes' famous poem, the hopes of many people still burn to a crisp while mass media keep cool.

Workers' Rights

Major media pundits have consistently encouraged the Democratic Party to back away from labor unions.

In early fall, when Bill Clinton momentarily balked in his support of a free trade pact with Mexico that could cost U.S. manufacturing jobs, pundits asked whether he was "too controlled by organized labor." In all the previous months that Clinton supported Mexican free trade, these commentators did not suggest he was "too controlled by big business."

In the media industry itself, mergers and economic recession have helped to undermine the bargaining power of workers. In many media workplaces, management's hostility toward unions is obvious. That atmosphere can affect the tone and content of news coverage.

Public broadcasting has been little better in presenting the perspectives of workers. Regular public TV shows that deal with economic matters—Louis Rukeyser's "Wall $treet Week," "Adam Smith's Money World" and the "Nightly Business Report"—are presented from the standpoint of investors, not employees.

Corporate Campaign Contributions

An exceptional PBS "Frontline" documentary aired a week before the election. "The Best Campaign Money Can Buy"—co-produced by the Center for Investigative Reporting—incisively probed the role of big money flowing to presidential candidates.

But that kind of reporting has been scarce. Coverage of campaign fundraising usually tallies dollar amounts as just one more aspect of the "horserace"—who's ahead, who's behind. Rarely do we learn what services the politician has rendered, or might render, in return for contributions.

It isn't the fault of news outlets that politicians try to dodge certain topics. But the evasion is mutual. Mainstream journalism has functioned in sync with politicians to define the limits of electoral discourse.

October 28, 1992

Part IX

Robertson, Perot and Other Saviors

Two shadows hanging over the 1996 presidential race, Pat Robertson and Ross Perot, are fond of denouncing the news media—even though they have artfully used media to establish themselves as power brokers in national politics. Whether Robertson, Perot and other would-be saviors are sublime or ridiculous depends on how you look at them.

Pat Robertson's Born-Again UPI?

- *"Sources tell United Press International that hidden Soviet missiles targeted against the U.S. are still inside Cuba."*

- *"George Bush is the individual responsible for exposing the sexual misdeeds of Rev. Jimmy Swaggart, UPI has learned."*

- *"Russia is planning to invade Israel, sources tell UPI. God will retaliate and destroy Russia with earthquakes and volcanoes."*

In fact, UPI did not dispatch any of these wild tales. But all three *were* reported in total earnestness by a man who is positioned to purchase the news service—televangelist Pat Robertson.

It's easy to chuckle at Rev. Robertson's claims, but it would be a mistake to laugh off his growing political and media power. The impending acquisition of UPI is just one more reason to take him seriously.

An astute businessman, Robertson is the most powerful and political of the televangelists. His "Christian Coalition" seeks to mobilize "pro-family" activists to take control of the Republican Party and ultimately the federal government. Robertson's media empire includes the Christian Broadcasting Network, the highly-profitable Family Channel cable network and various news/talk radio stations.

Calling himself a "white knight," Robertson says he wants to return UPI to its heyday, when it provided news copy to more than 700 newspapers and many broadcast stations. In the last decade UPI has looked more like a high wire act than a wire service, teetering on the edge of disaster with ownership changes, bankruptcies, staff layoffs and a shrinking client list.

Those who predict that a Robertson-owned UPI might be as journalistically independent as the church-owned *Christian Science Monitor* fail to understand the former (and perhaps future) presidential candidate. Robertson seeks nothing less than transformation of the U.S. government into one "controlled by God"; democracy, Robertson writes, is only "the next-best government."

A born-again UPI would be akin to the *Washington Times*, controlled by Rev. Sun Myung Moon's Unification Church. The right-wing newspaper loses big money, but wins legitimacy for the Moon organization—even after top editors of the paper, including the founding editor-in-chief, have resigned due to editorial interference by church officials.

Robertson's ownership of UPI may not mean overt meddling in the newsroom. Instead—as occurs at many media outlets whether corporate or church-owned—the well-known interests and biases of the owner may lead journalists to censor themselves.

News staffers at NBC, which is owned by General Electric, are well aware of GE's corporate interests: nuclear power, military contracts, etc. On several occasions, NBC journalists have sanitized reports to avoid offending their boss. One result: A "Today Show" segment on boycotts neatly ignored the biggest boycott in the country, the one targeted at GE.

But as politically active as GE is, it cares little about social issues such as abortion, gay rights, school textbooks and art censorship. Not so for Pat Robertson. You name the controversy, he has an opinion—usually a far-right one. He has supported South African apartheid and Guatemalan military dictators; he's called for ending Social Security and federal urban aid programs.

And Robertson doesn't hesitate to use his media clout. Week after week, his Christian Broadcasting Network mobilizes activists and money in support of Operation Rescue and other anti-abortion efforts. On the "700 Club" TV talk show which he hosts, Robertson denounces feminists as anti-child and anti-family.

Throughout the 1980s, CBN regularly lobbied on-air for military aid to El Salvador and the Nicaraguan Contra rebels. After Congress cut off aid to the Contras, the "700 Club" held a telethon to raise funds for them. A month later, the *Miami Herald* reported that CBN was the largest private donor to the Contras, which named one of its units the "Pat Robertson Brigade."

Given his heavy involvement in Central America, it's doubtful that a Robertson-owned UPI would aggressively pursue the news there. In the 1980s, UPI broke major stories linking the White House to Contra operations—after Congress had prohibited U.S. support. If Robertson had owned UPI then, would editors have gone ahead with these stories or would they have engaged in self-censorship?

Top UPI editors say they accept Robertson's pledge that he won't interfere in the newsroom. But his views are so well-known, he may not have to.

Years ago, staffers at Associated Press commonly hurled this putdown at their competitor: "UPI gets it first, AP gets it right."

If Robertson resurrects UPI, the new slogan might become: "UPI gets it first *and* gets it right…wing."

[Mercifully, Robertson's plan to buy UPI fell through.]

May 20, 1992

The World
According to Pat Robertson

One of the most bizarre power brokers of the Republican Party, evangelist Pat Robertson, recently sent out a remarkable fundraising letter.

No, the letter doesn't declare that Robertson's prayers saved his expensive broadcast studios from a hurricane. He made that claim back in 1985.

Nor does the letter accuse George Bush of being the hidden hand in exposing Rev. Jimmy Swaggart's sexual escapades. That charge was made in 1988, when Robertson was running against George Bush for president. Now running very much *with* Bush, Robertson is the key figure rallying fundamentalist Christians behind the Bush-Quayle ticket.

The recent letter is aimed at raising funds for the campaign opposing an equal rights amendment to Iowa's constitution. The measure, on the Iowa ballot in November, simply bars discrimination based on gender.

Ah, if only things were so simple. Rev. Robertson, however, is blessed with the ability to see the bigger picture—the hidden "feminist agenda." His letter spells out what the equal rights amendment is *really* about:

"It is about a socialist, anti-family political movement that encourages women to leave their husbands, kill their children, practice witchcraft, destroy capitalism and become lesbians."

WOW! All that in one amendment to a state constitution!

Since Robertson's explanation of the ERA uses about as many words as the whole Iowa amendment (a total of 27), we've decided to turn the tables on the politician-preacher.

Here's an analysis of what his letter is really about.

- *Socialist.* Rev. Robertson thinks that just about any government program aimed at helping people is "socialist." That's why he once called for an end to Social Security.

- *Anti-family political movement.* In the world according to Pat Robertson, any living arrangement that doesn't resemble "Father Knows Best" is a satanic plot.

- *Encourages women to leave their husbands.* Of course many women will tell you that leaving their husbands was the best thing they ever did. Imagine, for instance, what it would be like to stay married to a man with Pat Robertson's mentality.

- *Kill their children.* That's an ironic one. Robertson and his political allies aren't exactly sustaining young lives when they succeed in cutting social programs. Every time children go hungry or lose access to medical care, their health is jeopardized.

- *Practice witchcraft.* Maybe our country would be in better shape if we had a few Salem witch trials now and then. Perhaps we should start by putting a stake in the ground for Hillary Clinton.

- *Destroy capitalism.* No need for such worries. Capitalism is hardly in retreat these days. Pat Robertson might feel reassured after plunking down some rubles for a Big Mac the next time he's near Red Square in Moscow.

- *Become lesbians.* Rev. Robertson seems to be saying that unequal rights must be maintained in order to enforce heterosexual behavior. Does he believe that legal bias is needed to ensure that errant Americans straighten up and fly right?

Robertson's litany of feminist horrors may make you chuckle. But the televangelist is no joke. Unfortunately, few news outlets are probing his long-term plans.

Robertson's so-called Christian Coalition is growing fast, and now claims a quarter-million members. Its goal is to take over the Republican Party county-by-county, state-by-state, and then nationally within eight years. In over 20 states, Robertson has chapters in every county.

Operating "below radar" and aided by its tax-exempt status as a "social welfare organization," the Christian Coalition has quietly amassed a grassroots army. Its leaders talk of "getting the Christians out of the churches and into the precincts." They target low-turnout elections, believing that a disciplined minority is all that's needed to seize the political process.

President Bush's repeated concessions to right-wing demands this year were largely aimed at shoring up support from Robertson, while warding off the Patrick Buchanan challenge. Buchanan's "brigades" were puny and his campaign a non-starter because Robertson—who personally and politically scorns Bush—held his troops firmly in the president's camp.

Besides raising money for Stop ERA in Iowa, the Christian Coalition is giving support this fall to statewide ballot campaigns against gays in Oregon and Colorado. Backing Robertson's political endeavors is his Christian Broadcasting Network, which uses the airwaves to mobilize activists, lobby Congress and raise funds for causes such as abortion-clinic blockades, Guatemalan dictators and South African apartheid.

Pat Robertson may sound absurd, but he's no laughing matter.

September 9, 1992

H. Ross Perot:
The Ultimate Insider

No independent or third-party presidential candidate in recent history has received a bigger media boost than H. Ross Perot.

The billionaire has a huge budget for television ads, but he hasn't needed to spend a penny on TV yet, thanks to all the free promotional time he's received. In fact, Perot's candidacy has largely been a TV creation, from its launch on CNN's "Larry King Live" in February to follow-up appearances on "60 Minutes" and elsewhere.

Most of the TV interviews and profiles displayed a worship of money and power that might have made Robin Leach blush on "Lifestyles of the Rich and Famous": Gee whiz Mr. Perot, you're such a tough-talking straight-shooter!

In recent weeks, journalists have begun to take a harder look at Perot. But by this late date, Perot has gotten such a build-up as the savior for voters fed up with the status quo, he's able to accuse journalists of doing the establishment's bidding if they question him any more vigorously than Larry King did.

Unlike Perot, most independent presidential candidates in recent years have been heavily censored. A case in point was the 1980 third-party campaign of environmentalist Barry Commoner, who was the subject of glowing profiles in national media outlets...until he announced for president.

A true outsider, Commoner sought to tap voters' anger at a political system "taken over by big business." Besides voicing contempt, he offered well-thought-out programs for change. Thanks to mainstream media, Commoner ended up being "the best presidential candidate no one ever heard of."

Everyone's heard of H. Ross Perot. Unfortunately, most of what we've heard has been myth.

We've heard about the reluctant candidate who just happened to remark "off the cuff" to Larry King that he'd run for president if "the people" put his name on all 50 state ballots. In fact, as the weekly *Dallas Observer* reported, Perot arranged the King appearance after considering other possible media forums for his announcement, including the *Wall Street Journal.*

We've heard a lot about how Perot will attack our nation's problems by appointing teams of "world class experts," but little about his first campaign appointment: Admiral James Stockdale, chosen as interim vice presidential running-mate. While Stockdale has a record of courage in surviving years as a prisoner of war in Hanoi, he also has a history—which the national media have ignored—of involvement with right-wing groups such as the Rockford Institute.

The most absurd of the Perot myths is that he's an "outsider"—above the dirty dealing of government. In fact, much of Perot's fortune stems from his ability to milk government for contracts, subsidies and tax breaks. Perot was aptly dubbed "America's First Welfare Billionaire" in Michael Tomasky's devastating profile in the May 26, 1992 *Village Voice.*

Today, candidate Perot ridicules "these guys with their alligator shoes and their briefcases running up and down the halls getting their special deals cut." When Perot needed deals cut, he went straight to the top.

In September 1972, the Nixon Administration granted Perot's company a Medicare computerization contract—even though it was the *highest* of three bidders. Two months later, Perot's corporate deputies donated $200,000 to the Committee to Re-Elect the President (CREEP).

In 1973, Perot's company was outbid for a major computer contract in New York—but after a private meeting with Governor Nelson Rockefeller, Perot's firm got back into consideration and wound up with a consulting contract.

In 1980, Perot's firm seemingly lost a $2 billion Medicaid contract in Texas when a three-member hearing board voted unanimously for a competing firm. The decision was reversed after Perot twisted political arms in Texas, while generating a smear campaign in the media against the other company.

Besides manipulating government for his own ends, Perot has also been a policy insider—involved in some of the country's most hideous overseas adventures. In the early 1980s, Perot was a member of President Reagan's Foreign Intelligence Advisory Board, which oversaw the CIA. During Perot's watch, the CIA illegally mined Nicaragua's harbors, and produced a "Psychological Warfare" manual instructing the U.S.-backed Nicaraguan Contras to assassinate civilians.

Perot was a close ally of Richard Nixon in promoting the Vietnam War long after most Americans had turned against it. He maintained almost weekly contact with the White House, and had several private meetings with the president.

Perot says the meetings focused almost entirely on the issue of prisoners of war. But Nixon Administration memos tell a different story—that Perot once offered to spend $50 million for a PR campaign in support of Nixon and the war, and offered another $10 million to establish a pro-Nixon think tank. According to the memos, Nixon accepted both offers; neither was fulfilled.

While Perot was aggressively supporting Nixon's war effort, White House aides intervened on behalf of Perot's business interests with numerous federal agencies, including the IRS. White House memos referred to Perot as a "financial angel" who should be "stroked from time to time."

Former Nixon assistant Charles Colson commented recently: "I don't know anybody in the whole four years I was at the White House who was able to muscle himself in quicker into the president's own confidence." Another Nixon aide called Perot "the ultimate insider."

Ross Perot has reacted to the belated press scrutiny of his record by blaming negative coverage on a "Republican dirty tricks department." Given his history with Nixon, the Texas billionaire is an odd one to make such a charge.

May 27, 1992

Is Perot a "Watergate Waiting to Happen"?

Amid the thousands of words reported in the media about the 20th anniversary of the Watergate break-in, two were noticeably missing: Ross Perot.

In his attitudes toward democratic process and the press, Perot exhibits the same contempt, even paranoia, that brought down his friend Richard Nixon. A question begs to be asked: Is Perot a Watergate waiting to happen?

The Nixon White House went after its political enemies—especially journalists—with FBI probes, IRS audits, even FCC license challenges of "unfriendly" broadcasters.

Perot has never wielded federal power, but he's long had an affinity for the tactics—spying, threats, smears—that drove the Watergate scandal.

As the *Wall Street Journal* reported, Perot routinely hires former FBI agents and private detectives to investigate his adversaries. Political targets have included public officials and Vietnam veterans groups. And Perot's sleuths are not above using videotaped surveillance to probe for marital infidelities.

Perot seems to believe it's the role of government to cater to businessmen like him—and the role of the press to remain quiet and obedient. When journalists act as watchdogs, Perot doesn't just get mad, he gets even. In his hostility to the press, Perot is truly Nixonesque:

- **Blackmail:** In 1989, after the *Fort Worth Star-Telegram* published an article scrutinizing the business dealings of Perot's son, the paper's publisher says he received a bullying phone call from Perot in which the billionaire implied he possessed sexually compromising photos of a *Star-Telegram* employee and a city official. Perot admits he called the publisher, but denies any talk of photographs.

● **Innuendo:** In 1988, Dallas columnist Laura Miller reported that Perot had proposed the police cordon off black and Latino neighborhoods in South Dallas and conduct house-to-house searches for drugs and weapons. Such actions violate the Constitution's search and seizure protections. Asked about the report recently by the *New York Times*, Perot responded with his own question: "How much do you know about Laura Miller? Well, dig in… You just need to check her reputation for accuracy and professionalism."

● **I Never Said That:** Perot's main response to reporters is denial, no matter what the evidence. On the June 3, 1992 "Today Show," when co-host Katie Couric accurately quoted Perot's statement that he would not hire gays for certain Cabinet jobs, he replied: "You have completely misstated my positions." When Couric referred to a *Washington Post* op-ed article by Perot contradicting his current stance that he won't raise taxes, Perot claimed he'd been "taken out of context." Yet his article clearly states: "We must cut spending and raise taxes to pay our bills. We all know it."

● **Perotnoia:** In 1975, Perot undertook a secret mission to get the U.S. Congress to hand him $15 million in a special tax refund. The measure was quietly inserted into a major tax bill. (It failed to become law after the *Wall Street Journal* exposed the scheme, and the big bucks Perot had donated to Congress members who backed the proposal.) When National Public Radio anchor Linda Wertheimer recently interviewed Perot by phone about the tax rebate, he accused her of "doing a favor for somebody," and of engaging in a "classic setup." Then he questioned whether Wertheimer was a real journalist: "Is it really a radio program? You're not just somebody calling in?"

● **Can't Beat 'Em, Buy 'Em:** According to Nixon Administration memos from 1969, Perot once proposed a can-do plan to counter media coverage of the president and the Vietnam War: he offered to spend millions of dollars to purchase the ABC-TV network and the *Washington Star* newspaper. The plan was not carried out.

Perot did virtually buy his own biography— which he uses today to fend off journalistic probes about his beliefs and history. A testy Perot lectured Katie Couric, "There's all this interest in who I am and what I believe in. Read the book *On Wings of Eagles* by Ken Follett. It tells you all about me, more than you want to know." But there's a fact Perot didn't mention: He selected Follett to write the book, retaining control over its contents and the right to stop publication if it displeased him. It didn't. Perot is portrayed in heroic terms.

Back in April, the *New York Times* wrote—accurately— of a "largely uncritical press that has helped inflate [Perot's] achievements to near mythic proportions." In recent weeks, the press has examined Perot much more toughly—revealing that there is little the "can do" businessman "won't do" to win.

If he does win the White House, one wonders what actions he'll take against journalists who insist on being the public's watchdogs, and not Perot's lapdogs.

June 24, 1992

A True Outsider for President

After Ross Perot, who's next?

A few hints: Like Jimmy Carter, he has a background in the nuclear industry. But he's not aloof from the concerns of average Americans. He has the simplicity of a Ronald Reagan, the endearing gracelessness of a Gerald Ford, the ruddy countenance of a Richard Nixon, the bossy presence of an LBJ.

And best of all: He's no George Bush. Or Bill Clinton.

He's the ultimate outsider.

Give up?

Homer Simpson for President.

Some may object that he lacks the smarts of the current rage, H. Ross Perot. But have you ever listened closely to Perot for a few minutes? The guy made David Frost seem like a deep thinker. Anyway, who said making a couple of billion dollars is proof of brilliance?

Like the fellow in the Jerzy Kosinski novel and movie "Being There," both Perot and Simpson are comfortable on a TV screen. Somehow you just get comfortable, watching them.

Imagine how Bart's dad might become a major player in the '92 presidential race. Larry King has him on CNN. Homer Simpson lets drop near the end of the interview that he'd consider throwing his radiation-suit-hat in the ring, if sufficient adulation from viewers is forthcoming.

The response is enormous. The Twentieth Century Fox studio in Los Angeles is flooded with over a million calls—verified by the phone company!—by the next Thursday night. Matt Groening, the hidden hand behind the Simpsons, has a cow.

Journalists will attribute the Simpson-for-President phenomenon to the fact that millions of people are familiar with him and his reputed exploits, but few really know what he stands for. This is deemed somehow appropriate for the cartoonish campaign of 1992.

As with their treatment of Perot, numerous journalists will keep puffing Homer's candidacy, while lamenting that he never answers their questions.

When David Frost tries to pin him down in a follow-up interview, Homer Simpson's voice turns to the tone of knowing disdain that we recognize so fondly. As Frost persists, people tuning in grow indignant. Just who the hell does that Frost guy think he is? *Issues?* Come on. Issues suck.

Homer will rely heavily on his family for campaign spokespersons. Whatever one says about son Bart's shortcomings, at least he's never been implicated in the S&L scandal...unlike a current First Son. And the last thing Marge Simpson will do is offend—as Hillary Clinton has—millions of women who work at home, running a household.

When it comes to this year's fixation on which candidate best understands the suffering of America's middle class—in a race against a career politician from Arkansas, and a millionaire and a billionaire from Texas—Homer wins in a landslide.

You may object that this is all fantasy...in sharp contrast to the real political world. But let's remember that in the "real world," the Vice President of the United States recently took on Murphy Brown, a fictional TV character.

In fact, although hardly noticed by the political press corps, a fight between George Bush and Homer Simpson has been simmering since January 1992. That's when Bush attacked Homer's TV show in a speech to the National Religious Broadcasters' convention: "The nation needs to be closer to the Waltons than the Simpsons."

Son Bart responded instantly in a "Simpsons" episode, defending his family: "We *are* like the Waltons. We're praying for the end of the depression, too."

In 1990, when Barbara Bush called the TV show "the dumbest thing I've ever seen," she immediately received a letter of protest from Marge Simpson.

"We're far from perfect," read the note from the prospective First Lady. "But I try to teach my children always to give someone the benefit of the doubt and not talk badly about them, even if they are rich."

In any event, let's not assume that something can't happen here just because it initially seems absurd. Look at the Perot campaign, a media creation if ever there was one.

So don't rule out the head of America's most colorful prime-time household.

Of course the centerpiece of Homer Simpson's platform will be "family values." When a political system has grown this dysfunctional, it's the only way.

June 10, 1992

Pat Buchanan:
TV Pundit Wants to Be
President

When Patrick Buchanan joined the Republican presidential contest, the TV commentator and columnist entered two races at once. In the first, he found himself chasing after President Bush. But just as fast, he had to run away from David Duke while embracing his issues.

Although Buchanan and Duke ended up in the same place—using nearly identical rhetoric to challenge Bush from the right—they took totally different paths en route to becoming Republican presidential candidates. Duke rose to prominence through the use of KKK robes; Buchanan rode a more conventional vehicle—television.

To the political press corps, Duke is outside the mainstream. By contrast, Buchanan is one of the boys. Among TV pundits, he's been the leader of the pack—the first to appear on national TV seven days a week, as co-host of CNN's "Crossfire," host of CNN's "Capital Gang," and a regular member of the "McLaughlin Group." Besides these recurring gigs, he's a frequent guest on such programs as ABC's "Nightline" and "Good Morning America."

Buchanan's TV colleagues responded to "Pat's candidacy" largely with good-natured jesting. Pundits speak of Buchanan as a swell guy, not a Duke-like threat to liberties or racial groups: "I'm very fond of him" (Jack Germond); "a very civil, even a very kind, man" (Al Hunt); "a really nice guy; actually, a sweet person" (Fred Barnes).

Buchanan has served up his far-right positions so incessantly, they've become almost commonplace. His fellow TV pundits appear incapable of noticing the stark similarities in the ideologies of Buchanan and Duke.

Like Duke, Buchanan has for years displayed authoritarian and, yes, fascist inclinations. In his autobiography, *Right from the Beginning*, Buchanan waxes nostalgic about his dad's hero, General Francisco Franco of Spain. Franco and Chile's General Augusto Pinochet were military dictators who terminated democracy in their countries; in a 1989 column, Buchanan called them "soldier-patriots."

For years Buchanan championed accused Nazi war criminals, and campaigned for the U.S. Justice Department to stop "running down 70-year-old camp guards." He has questioned the historical record about the gassing of Jews at Treblinka. His columns have run in pro-Nazi publications that claim the death camps are a Jewish hoax.

In a bizarre 1977 column, Buchanan said that despite Hitler's anti-Semitic and genocidal tendencies, "he was also an individual of great courage…. Hitler's success was not based on his extraordinary gifts alone. His genius was an intuitive sense of the mushiness, the character flaws, the weakness masquerading as morality that was in the hearts of the statesmen who stood in his path."

While an aide to President Reagan in 1985, Buchanan was credited with scripting the chilling words the president used to defend his visit to the Bitburg cemetery, where dozens of Nazi SS troops were buried: The German soldiers were "victims just as surely as the victims in the concentration camps."

Three years later, when American Jewish leaders protested the building of a convent at Auschwitz, Buchanan denounced New York's Cardinal John O'Connor for criticizing anti-Semitism among Catholics: "If U.S. Jewry takes the clucking appeasement of the Catholic cardinalate as indicative of our submission, it is mistaken."

The commentator-turned-campaigner doesn't just have a Jewish problem. Like Duke, he has a black problem as well, having opposed every civil rights law and court decision for the past 30 years.

And Buchanan has a Martin Luther King obsession. When he was an editorial writer at the *St. Louis Globe-Democrat* in the 1960s, Buchanan took FBI memos smearing King and published them as his own editorials. In 1969, then-presidential adviser Buchanan implored Richard Nixon not to visit "the widow King" on the first anniversary of her husband's assassination: "Dr. King is one of the most divisive men in contemporary history."

Buchanan has an attraction to white-supremacist views. While in the Nixon White House, he called an *Atlantic* magazine article about the genetic basis of intelligence "a seminal piece of major significance for U.S. society." The piece, he wrote in a memo to Nixon, indicates that "integration of blacks and whites—but even more so, poor and well-to-do—is less likely to result in accommodation than it is in perpetual friction, as the incapable are placed consciously by government side by side with the capable."

Buchanan was one of the first to advocate that the Republican Party exploit racial issues. In another memo to Nixon, he wrote: "The time has come to say—we have done enough for the poor blacks; right now we want to give some relief for working-class ethnics and Catholics—and make an unabashed appeal to these patient working people, who always get the short end of the stick. If we can give 50 Phantoms to the Jews, and a multibillion dollar welfare program for the blacks...why not help the Catholics save their collapsing school system."

In 1989, Buchanan was still at it, castigating George Bush for currying the favor of Coretta King. In a series of columns, he argued that Reagan had done so much for blacks that civil rights groups should "close up shop." Meanwhile, Buchanan continued to defend South Africa—which he admiringly referred to as the "Boer Republic": "Why are Americans collaborating in a UN conspiracy to ruin her with sanctions?"

As a presidential candidate, Buchanan has couched many of his campaign themes, from trade policy to the "underclass," in racial terms. During a discussion of immigration, he asked contemptuously whether "Zulus" or "Englishmen" would be easier to assimilate.

Buchanan is also contemptuous of what he calls "the democratist temptation, the worship of democracy as a form of governance." The would-be president wrote: "Like all idolatries, democratism substitutes a false god for the real, a love of process for a love of country." He has written disparagingly of "the one man, one vote Earl Warren system."

In a 1991 column he suggested that "quasi-dictatorial rule" might be the solution to the problems of big municipalities and the federal fiscal crisis: "If the people are corrupt, the more democracy, the worse the government."

Buchanan's tactics have sometimes matched his antidemocratic philosophy: During Watergate he encouraged Nixon to "burn the tapes." He criticized Reagan for failing to simply pardon Oliver North.

During campaign '92, Buchanan's attempts to distance himself from David Duke are ironic. (He repeatedly complained that Republican officials treated him "no different than Duke.") Three years earlier, when Duke ran for the Louisiana legislature and shared a phone with the Klan, Buchanan ridiculed national Republican leaders for overreacting to Duke and his Nazi "costume": "Take a hard look at Duke's portfolio of winning issues, and expropriate those not in conflict with GOP principles."

Buchanan wrote that Duke was right on target attacking "reverse discrimination against white folks" and crime committed by the "urban underclass"—Buchanan's codephrase for blacks. He saluted Duke for walking "into the vacuum left when conservative Republicans in the Reagan years were intimidated into shucking off winning social issues."

Vintage Buchanan, the column concluded: "The GOP is throwing away a winning hand, and David Duke is only the first fellow to pick up the discards."

Buchanan is the second fellow to pick up the discards. When will the media pundits notice that these two men are playing substantially the same hand?

February 6, 1992

Part X
Covering U.S. Power Abroad

News reports are supposed to provide us with a window on the world, but often the pane is tinted red-white-and-blue. When conflict overseas involves United States military or diplomatic intervention, a closed loop of media coverage seldom allows much dissent or critical scrutiny. Truth is the first casualty, and rarely seems to recover.

War Crimes and the U.S. Media: The Case of El Salvador

When it comes to the actions of foes like Saddam Hussein, or the savage war in the former Yugoslavia, the phrase "war crimes" is frequently invoked by U.S. mass media.

By contrast, a gruesome war was waged for over a decade in El Salvador by a regime that Washington steadily armed and financed—yet the "war crimes" tag has been missing in action.

The war ended in 1991, after the United Nations helped negotiate a truce between the government and El Salvador's FMLN revolutionary movement. In the wake of findings by the U.N.'s Truth Commission on El Salvador, the Salvadoran regime's murder of nearly 70,000 civilians has recently received the intense, blunt coverage in U.S. media that was so rare in past years.

Here's a tiny bit of the ugly history:

** In March 1980, Archbishop Oscar Romero was assassinated on orders of Roberto D'Aubuisson, a U.S.-trained military officer who founded the ARENA party that still rules the country.

** In December 1980, four U.S. church women working with the poor in El Salvador were abducted, sexually abused and murdered by Salvadoran National Guardsmen. The abduction was ordered by military superiors. United States officials like then-Secretary of State Alexander Haig and U.N. Ambassador Jeane Kirkpatrick offered fraudulent excuses for the murders.

** Throughout the decade, the Salvadoran government assassinated students, clergy, peasants and union organizers. Most military commanders were involved in atrocities, and most were trained by the U.S.

** In November 1989, six priests and their two house-keepers were executed on the grounds of the Jesuit University by members of the elite, U.S.-trained Atlacatl Battalion on orders of Salvadoran military leaders.

Parallel to the bloody history of sustained war crimes was a history of cowardice and cover-up on the part of various U.S. media: News coverage of El Salvador was often shaped to conform more with Washington lies than with reports from human rights experts and journalists in the field.

Indeed, had powerful media outlets fought for the truth instead of succumbing to official fiction, many of these war crimes—paid for by U.S. taxpayers—could have been averted.

● In January 1982, *New York Times* journalist Ray Bonner reported on a massacre of hundreds of children, women and men in El Mozote carried out by the Atlacatl Battalion. After Washington denied there'd been a massacre and the Reagan administration launched a smear campaign against Bonner, the *Times* pulled him out of El Salvador. (A 1982 *Wall Street Journal* editorial slurring Bonner complained: "Communist sources were given greater credence than either the U.S. government or the government it was supporting.")

Bonner's reporting has been totally vindicated by the U.N. Truth Commission, which excavated the mass graves. But the cowardly removal of Bonner by *Times* executives in 1982 sent a powerful message to mainstream U.S. journalists who stayed behind in El Salvador: Reporting the facts—when they conflict with Washington—can cost you your job.

● In February 1988, *New York Times* correspondent James LeMoyne (who had taken over Bonner's old beat) wrote a vivid account of an El Salvador atrocity—the public execution of two peasants by FMLN guerrillas. But the event never occurred. It had been invented by a Salvadoran army propaganda officer and placed in a right-wing San Salvador newspaper—which LeMoyne read and reported as fact. It took six months of petitioning before the *Times* would even acknowledge the error.

● Throughout the 1980s, news reports in U.S. media regularly used euphemisms to describe El Salvador. The government was referred to as a "democracy" or a "fledgling democracy." Military leaders who assassinated priests were termed "moderates." Reporters spoke of "a civil war that has claimed 70,000 lives"— when they knew from briefings at the San Salvador Archdiocese human rights office that over 90 percent of the dead were not battle casualties, but civilians killed by government security forces and allied death squads. In deference to Washington, news accounts referred to "human rights abuses on both sides"— when evidence showed them running about 30 to 1 toward the government.

● In June 1989, while dozens of U.S. reporters trekked through San Salvador alongside visiting Vice President Dan Quayle, Salvadoran labor leader Jose Mazariego was abducted and tortured in another part of the city by military police. Although Mazariego's torture (he flew to Washington a week later and showed his wounds to members of Congress) was thoroughly reported in some papers, including *Newsday*, it was not mentioned in the *New York Times*…until Dan Quayle wrote a guest column a month later, dismissing the crime as "the brief detention and alleged mistreatment of a pro-FMLN union leader."

● One of the most important places to debate U.S. policy is the *Washington Post* op-ed page. During the 1980s there was no room on that page for the respected Americas Watch organization, which scrutinized human rights abuses in El Salvador and other U.S.-backed countries. *Post* editors deemed Americas Watch too *biased*—but published several articles by Helsinki Watch, its sister group that scrutinized abuses in Soviet-backed countries. The only time Americas Watch appeared prominently on the *Washington Post* op-ed page during the decade was when Jeane Kirkpatrick, a regular *Post* columnist, savaged the group.

Some members of Congress are hoping to launch a truth commission to investigate what White House officials knew about atrocities committed by their Salvadoran allies.

What's also needed is a commission of journalists to probe the reasons why national media outlets in the United States failed to blow the whistle on a terrorist regime financed by U.S. taxpayers.

April 14, 1993

BILL GENTILE FOR NEWSWEEK

ïstiani: *Man of the moment or second fiddle?*

BILL GENTILE FOR NEWSWEEK

Shock politics: *A victim of the FMLN*

Photographic Bias: *Newsweek* editors chose these two photos—El Salvador's huggable rightwing leader Alfredo Cristiani, juxtaposed with a victim of leftwing violence—to accompany its article, "The Return of the Right" (3/29/89). The article's bias mirrored the photos: *Newsweek* called Cristiani, head of a death squad-allied party, "the pleasant, democratic candidate," while warning that "an American pullout" would "almost surely result in a Marxist victory." In 1993, the U.N. Truth Commission blamed the U.S.-backed Salvadoran government for committing nearly all of the atrocities against civilians.

Best Liar in a Supporting Role

If you watched the 1993 Oscar presentations, you saw the award for best documentary feature go to "The Panama Deception." It's a powerful movie exposing that much of what the Pentagon—and national media—told us about the U.S. invasion of Panama was false.

One of the movie's "stars" appears and reappears throughout the documentary to offer the Pentagon line on the invasion. He tells us that few Panamanian civilians were killed; that there were no mass graves; that keeping reporters from the invasion was purely unintentional. Each of these claims is quickly debunked by eyewitnesses and other filmed documentation.

The Pentagon spokesman with the forked tongue was Pete Williams—who later became famous for his PR role in "Desert Storm."

Oscar day was a big one in the life of Pete Williams, but not because of his part in an Academy Award-winning film. That same day, he had something different to celebrate: he began his job as NBC-TV's newest national correspondent. Working out of NBC's Washington bureau, Williams will be a "general assignment" news reporter.

As the Pentagon's chief spokesperson for years, Williams specialized in peddling falsehoods and half-truths to reporters and the public about the Panama invasion and the Gulf War. He was a key player in orchestrating the censorship of news coverage of the U.S. military overseas, including the practice of herding journalists into "press pools" that could be kept away from the action.

In John R. MacArthur's definitive book *Second Front: Censorship and Propaganda in the Gulf War*, Pete Williams is the commander of "Operation Desert Muzzle." Williams is shown to be almost allergic to the truth, an individual who routinely deceived reporters about how much access they'd be granted and about what was happening "on the ground." According to MacArthur, "Pete lied to me count-less times while I was researching my book"; one of Williams' whoppers was "his preposterous figure of 457 Iraqi dead" during the war.

With his years of success in thwarting freedom of the press, Williams might seem an odd choice to become a network TV journalist protecting "the public's right to know." A reporter's mission, after all, should be ferreting out official deceptions and cover-ups.

But given that his new employer is NBC, it's actually a fitting choice. That network was a willing partner of Pete Williams during the Gulf War—more engaged in cheerlead-ing for the Pentagon than journalism for the public.

During the war, NBC anchor Tom Brokaw questioned whether reporters had a right to cover the return of dead soldiers, asking: "Do you think that's in the best interest of the U.S.?"

When a British journalist tried to report on the war independent of the Pentagon's press pool that Williams had helped establish, NBC correspondent Brad Willis informed on the reporter to the U.S. Marines.

Midway into the war, NBC News acquired dramatic footage from video journalist Jon Alpert showing that U.S. bombing had devastated Iraqi civilian districts in Basra, the country's second-largest city, and elsewhere. NBC News president Michael Gartner not only suppressed the video-tape, he forbade Alpert—who'd worked for NBC on and off for a dozen years—from ever working there again.

Throughout the war, correspondents for NBC (and other networks) expressed reverence for U.S. weapons: While one NBC reporter referred to the Iraqi Scud as "an evil weapon," another described a U.S. missile as "accurate to within a few feet"—even after acknowledging that one of those "accurate" weapons had just struck a housing com-pound.

Repeating erroneous information put out by Williams and the Pentagon, Tom Brokaw hailed the Patriot—inaccurately—as "the missile that put the Iraqi Scud in its place." What Brokaw didn't report is that NBC's owner, General Electric, produces parts for the Patriot and dozens of other weapons used against Iraq. In fact, GE made a financial killing in the war.

So Pete Williams should feel quite at home at NBC. He's jumped from one end of the military/industrial/media complex to the other.

Ever since General Electric took over NBC in the mid-1980s, it has been eliminating seasoned journalists in an effort to save money. Perhaps NBC News should take the final cost-cutting step: Replace all its journalists with government publicists, and simply report as gospel the press releases that come spitting out of the Pentagon and other official agencies.

[*Note: One of the authors of this column, Jeff Cohen, appears briefly as a media critic in "The Panama Deception."*]

March 31, 1993

When Dying Children
Aren't Newsworthy

Two years ago, on Jan. 16, 1991, the United States launched the first missiles of the Persian Gulf War. Since then we've heard little about Iraqi children, who have been dying in large numbers.

Rather than examining the deadly aftermath of the war, U.S. media outlets have much preferred to reiterate the need for retribution against Saddam Hussein. As the headline over a *New York Times* editorial declared last July: "Time to Punish Hussein—Again."

One of the enduring media myths of the Gulf War is the idea that wars are fought not against countries, but against individual rulers. The endless repetition of "punish Saddam" themes has served to obscure the impacts of the Gulf War on Iraqi civilians, and to justify the present embargo against Iraq. Yet Iraq's dictator has not suffered. Iraq's children have.

A few months ago, the *New England Journal of Medicine* [Sept. 24, 1992] published a study which concluded that "the Gulf War and trade sanctions caused a threefold increase in mortality among Iraqi children under 5 years of age. We estimate that an excess of more than 46,900 children died between January and August 1991."

The researchers refuted the Pentagon's favorite distortion. "During the Gulf War, it was suggested that by using high-precision weapons with strategic targets, the Allied forces were producing only limited damage to the civilian population. The results of our study contradict this claim and confirm that the casualties of war extend far beyond those caused directly by warfare."

Such information is not new. In the spring and fall of 1991, a pair of task forces—composed of Harvard Study Team physicians and other scientists—reported that childhood mortality had soared after bombing destroyed much of Iraq's infrastructure. The country faced lethal shortages of food, electricity, sewage treatment, potable water and basic health care.

Another independent group, the U.S.-based Physicians for Human Rights, warned in summer 1991 that "Iraq's hospitals are overwhelmed with children under 5 who are severely ill from cholera, typhoid, infectious hepatitis, dysentery, and other diarrheal diseases."

These reports have drawn only fleeting media coverage in the United States. Meanwhile, there has been no shortage of heart-wrenching journalism about the brutal suppression of Kurds by the Baghdad government. The *New York Times Magazine*, for example, featured the subject in its first cover story of 1993, "Iraq Accused: A Case of Genocide."

In contrast, U.S. news media rarely even mention the Iraqi children who continue to die largely because of the Gulf War and sanctions still in place against Iraq.

A rare exception appeared—sort of—in the *New York Times* recently. A Dec. 27, 1992 news story provided graphic details about health effects of the war and embargo, including eyewitness accounts of post-war Iraq from U.S. physicians in the Medicine for Peace organization. However, the newspaper published the 1,443-word article only in its Long Island edition!

The vast majority of *Times* readers did not see the unusual article, which quoted Dr. Michael Viola—director of oncology at University Hospital at Stony Brook on Long Island—denouncing the current United Nations embargo against Iraq. "Although Americans have been told that the embargo exempts medical supplies and that the lack of supplies may be caused by the military's diverting them from the public," the article reported, Dr. Viola flatly disputed the claim.

"Along with the International Red Cross and UNICEF, we follow the shipments coming in of the medicines and supplies," he said. "We found that only 5 percent of the need is coming into the country. The fact remains that because of this situation many children have died and more continue to die."

The Long Island-quarantined article ended with a quote from Dr. Viola: "There needs to be a restructuring of the United States embargo to allow for food and medical supplies and to separate Saddam Hussein from the Iraqi children."

But U.S. news coverage has failed to distinguish between Saddam Hussein and Iraqi civilians. The dictator's satanic media image has loomed so large that it has prevented us from glimpsing the humanity of Iraqi people— caught in a vise between the repressive Baghdad regime and the ongoing U.N. sanctions spearheaded by the United States.

Health conditions inside Iraq improved only a bit during 1992. As a new year begins, the situation remains grim. Available figures indicate that about 100,000 Iraqis under age 5 have died as a result of the war and the embargo. Though you'll rarely encounter a word about them in American news media, more are dying every day.

January 6, 1993

Somalia:
The Unasked Questions

Most Americans have followed the U.S. military intervention in Somalia on television, seeing the Marines land in full camera glare, and watching as they move deeper into the country's starving interior.

On television, Somalia is a series of dramatic images. It's not that TV is unable to provide history and context. But such background would raise troubling questions that TV networks—and other national media—might find difficult to answer.

● *What took the U.S. media so long?*

In January 1991, six of the world's leading relief agencies warned that millions of Africans—mainly in Somalia, Sudan and Ethiopia—might starve unless food aid was forthcoming. In the fall of 1991, the United Nations warned of grave food shortages for millions of Somalis.

Huge story, right? The kind of calamity the world's richest country needed to know about? That's not how the TV networks saw it. In all of 1991, Somalia received a total of three minutes on the three nightly news shows.

In July 1991, the media watch group FAIR published a cover story in its magazine, "Hunger In Africa: A Story Untold Until Too Late." The report was aimed as a wake-up call for the thousands of journalists who receive the magazine.

But most media continued to snooze.

From January to July of 1992, when U.S. media finally began to notice starvation in Somalia, the country received a mere 11 minutes of evening network coverage. By then, perhaps as many as 20 percent of Somalis under age 5 had died, according to relief experts.

When isolationists blamed the stark TV famine footage in the autumn of 1992 for ensnaring the U.S. into its Somalian commitment, they turned reality upside down. The U.S. media spent months ignoring the murderous tragedy of Somalia—long after it was being prominently covered in Europe and elsewhere.

Food aid is now desperately needed in Sudan, Mozambique and Liberia. It shouldn't take the deployment of U.S. Marines before American TV networks report these stories.

● *Did Washington help cause the problem?*

To watch "Operation Restore Hope" on TV is to see the U.S. in white hats, riding in to rescue the starving people of Africa. Most viewers wouldn't know that the U.S. government contributed to the Somali catastrophe by arming a vicious dictator, Mohamed Siad Barre, for most of his 21-year reign.

If "Iraqgate" describes Washington's decade-long alliance with Saddam Hussein, how about "Somaligate"?

While the Reagan Administration was dispatching military aid to Siad Barre in 1988, the dictator engaged in a counterinsurgency campaign that slaughtered some 50,000 Somali civilians and forced a half-million refugees into exile, according to Human Rights Watch.

Using a divide-and-rule strategy, Siad Barre pitted clan against clan. After his dictatorship was deposed in January 1991, the legacy of clan fighting continued, contributing in a big way to today's famine. Indeed, the clan most ravaged by starvation is the one that lived adjacent to Siad Barre's clan and had much of its fertile land stolen during the dictatorship.

Reporting from New York on the eve of the Marine landing in Somalia, ABC anchor Peter Jennings offered a brief background report on how Washington armed the Somali dictator as a Cold War gambit to keep neighboring Soviet-backed Ethiopia tied down in a war: "Millions of innocent people paid the price." Unlike Jennings, anchors

Dan Rather and Tom Brokaw "parachuted" into Somalia—more interested in on-the-ground action coverage than in history.

No TV network has focused on another factor contributing to African hunger: the role of the International Monetary Fund and big Western banks in steering African agriculture away from local sustenance to export crops, like tobacco.

And from mainstream media, one wouldn't know that Western aid to Africa is far less than what Western interests take out of Africa in profits and income on loans. The continent's foreign debt stands at $235 billion, and is growing.

● *Were the Marines the only option?*

Among TV pundits, the question is almost beyond debate: A full-scale U.S. military operation was the only way to "save Somalia." What pundits don't say is that many relief experts wanted a multinational United Nations force to intervene—not the U.S. acting virtually alone.

U.S. diplomats repeatedly blocked major deployments of U.N. peacekeeping troops in Somalia and other African countries. One way Washington obstructs the U.N. is by refusing to pay its financial obligations: a total of $415 million is owed, $120 million of that for peacekeeping missions.

A fully-funded U.N. force, including troops from Islamic nations, might have a better chance of digging in for the long haul to help rebuild civil society in this Muslim country.

Why does TV, our dominant medium, find it so difficult to examine basic aspects of history and policy? The deeper answers to that question will probably not be televised.

December 16, 1992

A Tale of Two Terrorists:
Theirs Versus Ours

To hear the Bush Administration and U.S. media tell it, there is no government conduct more reprehensible than the coddling of terrorists who've blown up civilian airliners and murdered innocent people.

In the bombing of Pan Am Flight 103 over Lockerbie, Scotland, the accused government is Libya. Leading the prosecution is the United States. Unless Libya quickly surrenders two alleged plane bombers, economic sanctions may be imposed by the United Nations.

Editorials in major American newspapers have praised President Bush's stance and called for aggressive U.S. action against Libya. Columnist William Safire wants more than sanctions; he has urged Bush to take military action against Qaddafi, who "harbors his killer terrorists." (Safire's advice to Bush was part of a three-point plan to win reelection in November.)

The only question raised by U.S. media is whether Syria was absolved of involvement in the Lockerbie massacre as a payoff for becoming a U.S. ally in the war against Iraq.

But a bigger issue has been totally ignored: **hypocrisy**.

As many journalists know, the U.S. government also has a history of protecting jet-bombing terrorists. George Bush himself has played a role in coddling such terrorists. But these facts have gone unmentioned in all the coverage of Libya and Lockerbie.

The parallels are disturbing. The two accused Libyan terrorists were government officials. "Our" two terrorists— Orlando Bosch and Luis Posada Carriles—often worked closely with the CIA.

Their two allegedly waged a war against Western infidels. "Our" two killed and maimed in the fight against satanic Communism, especially Cuba. All terrorists—whether theirs or ours—kill innocent people in the name of the great crusade.

The U.S. media have denounced their two alleged terrorists, but lately have gone mum about "our" two. Here's the rest of the story.

In 1990 George Bush's Justice Department freed right-wing Cuban terrorist Orlando Bosch from a Miami jail, even though U.S. authorities acknowledged he'd engaged in dozens of bombings—including the October 1976 bombing of a civilian Cuban airliner that killed 73 people. The plane blew up soon after taking off from Barbados en route to Jamaica and Havana.

Bosch was freed after intense lobbying aimed at the White House by prominent Florida Republicans—including Senator Connie Mack, Representative Ileana Ros-Lehtinen and the president's son Jeb Bush. The U.S. has steadfastly refused to turn Bosch over to Cuba for trial.

Bosch has a long history of violence. In 1968, he was convicted of firing a bazooka at a Polish freighter in Miami harbor. In 1974, Bosch violated his parole after being subpoenaed in a murder case, and fled to Latin America. There, he and other CIA veterans formed the terrorist group CORU, which launched a bombing spree across the hemisphere, including the downing of the Cuban passenger jet. Though never convicted of that crime, Bosch spent a decade in Venezuelan prisons.

When the U.S. Justice Department granted parole to the former parole-violator two years ago, Bosch flagrantly pledged to continue meeting with Cuban militants even though this violated his parole arrangement. Lately, extremist Cubans aren't restricting their violence to foreign planes, boats and embassies; they've targeted the homes of Cuban-Americans who they feel are too soft on Castro.

Bosch's partner in crime was Luis Posada, who worked for the CIA for years in the 1960s. Posada was trained in explosives by the CIA, and—along with Bosch—

reputedly masterminded the airline bombing.

Since that bombing was perpetrated by a number of CIA veterans, the agency knew instantly that Posada, Bosch and accomplices were involved. But the CIA—headed by George Bush at the time—did nothing to bring the men to justice.

In 1985, Posada escaped from prison in Venezuela where he was being prosecuted for the jet bombing. Instead of returning the escaped terrorist to justice, the U.S. apparently found him a job in El Salvador as one of the directors of the operation to resupply the Nicaraguan Contras. Posada was recruited to the Contra program and supervised by longtime CIA operative Felix Rodriguez, who—during this period—reported regularly to Vice President Bush's office.

In 1986, when major U.S. newspapers identified Posada as being a Contra overseer in El Salvador, did the U.S. move to apprehend the terrorist still wanted in Venezuela today? No, he was allowed to disappear again.

When President Bush talks tough about sanctions against Libya for harboring jet-bombing terrorists while he has been protecting U.S. operatives and associates who performed similar acts, that is an exercise in hypocrisy.

It doesn't say much for U.S. media that they allow him to get away with it.

April 8, 1992

M. WUERKER

Skewed Coverage
of the Middle East

Reporting on the historic Mideast peace talks in Madrid, many U.S. journalists managed to depart from time-worn cliches and stereotypes about Israelis and Palestinians. But much of the underlying news spin remained all too familiar.

The current media script may not cast Israeli leaders as beleaguered heroes of the Middle East drama—but U.S. officials are still the white-hat paragons of virtue. This scripting serves the White House, but not independent journalism.

Repeatedly portrayed as "honest brokers," President Bush and Secretary of State James Baker came off as above-the-fray in Madrid—anguished parents beseeching fractious children to listen to reason and settle their quarrels peacefully. *USA Today* echoed many other credulous page-one headlines: "BUSH URGES MIDEAST BALANCE."

Countless news stories explained that Bush spoke as a peacemaker. "Mr. Bush sought to strike a balance in his address" (*New York Times*) "in a measured speech" (*USA Today*). Yet Bush's speech did not urge Israel to trade land for peace, a concept embodied in U.N. resolutions which the president himself cited as the basis for negotiations. Nor did Bush criticize Israeli expansion of settlements in the West Bank.

Casting the U.S. government as a benevolent arbitrator or innocent bystander amounts to PR flackery for the White House. And it well serves the Israeli government, which continues to receive vital subsidies from Uncle Sam even while complaining that his loyalty is wavering.

The myth of American neutrality in the Israeli-Palestinian conflict requires downplaying the U.S. government's massive aid pipeline to Israel—a billion dollars every few months—which went virtually unmentioned amid the millions of words from Madrid that came off American presses and transmitters.

A *Wall Street Journal* front page was typical in mentioning only housing-loan guarantees for Israel, delayed by Bush, as the ultimate U.S. "lever" over Israel. However, with enormous largess from American tax dollars continually subsidizing Israel as it occupies the West Bank and Gaza Strip, the U.S. government has an option which U.S. news media refuse to acknowledge: a cutoff of aid to the occupiers.

With the Madrid conference over, most Palestinians living in the occupied territories cannot hope to match the image of Palestinian spokeswoman Hanan Ashrawi, described by *New York Newsday* as having "clipped English, stylishly short hair and an impish smile"—in pointed contrast to the P.L.O. chief, "the gesticulating and bug-eyed Yasser Arafat, with his 5 o'clock shadow, military costume and black-and-white headdress." Ashrawi's manners may play well in New York and Peoria, but perhaps we should get used to the idea that Palestinians who dress and speak differently are also worth listening to.

One expert apparently worth listening to is Martin Indyk, director of the Washington Institute for Near East Policy, closely tied to the pro-Israel lobby. Indyk, profusely praising Baker, was the only Mideast analyst quoted in the *New York Times* edition wrapping up coverage from Madrid. CNN presented him as one of its regular and purportedly independent experts during the Madrid conference. [In 1993 Indyk went on to become a special assistant to President Clinton and "senior director for Near East and South Asian Affairs" of the National Security Council.]

Way before Madrid, the TV networks had made a star out of Benjamin Netanyahu—the telegenic and combative deputy foreign minister who is Israel's answer to Elliott Abrams, the former State Department official who pled guilty to lying to Congress under oath. Like Abrams, the more he's off (factually), the more he's on (TV).

When Israeli police killed 17 Palestinians at Jerusalem's Al-Aqsa Mosque in October 1990, Netanyahu led a disinformation blitz asserting that the Palestinians were killed after they'd rioted and pelted Jewish worshippers from above the Wailing Wall with huge stones. At the time, Netanyahu's fable dominated much of the U.S. media. Later even the official Israeli inquiry debunked Netanyahu's account and blamed police for starting the clash.

Netanyahu and other Israeli officials have reason to be pleased that U.S. media so often accept their mapping of the region. The "MacNeil/Lehrer NewsHour," for example, presented an Oct. 29, 1991 report in which Jim Lehrer matter-of-factly referred to "the security zone in southern Lebanon." Projected behind him was a map with the south of Lebanon only marked ISRAELI SECURITY ZONE, without quotation marks.

News maps in the *New York Times* have rendered the 400-square-mile Israeli occupation of southern Lebanon invisible. And on a number of occasions in 1991 the *Times* published a map showing the Golan Heights as part of Israel—and not among lands "occupied by Israel"—despite the fact that Israel's annexation of the Golan has no international recognition.

An improvement in media coverage out of Madrid was a new bluntness in reporting on Yitzhak Shamir's past. The Israeli prime minister had vetoed formal P.L.O. participation in Madrid because he wouldn't talk with "terrorists." Some press outlets abandoned their usual euphemisms and mentioned that during the 1940s Shamir had been active in "Jewish terrorist organizations" such as the Irgun, and its most extreme faction, the Stern Gang, which assassinated British officials and others.

At the Madrid conference Netanyahu and Shamir gained a lot of media attention when they said that certain Arab leaders sided with Hitler in World War Two. The charge is true. But news reports hardly mentioned the fact that Shamir was a leading figure in the Stern Gang when it sent communiqués to Hitler applauding his totalitarian principles and proposing an alliance with the Third Reich against the British.

Meanwhile, in an era when America's mass media and government officials herald democratic changes in Eastern Europe, and independence achieved by Lithuanians, Estonians and Latvians, there is no democratic imperative cited for Palestinians—and no comparable use of the "pro-democracy" label for the Palestinian quest for self-determination.

With the klieg lights turned off in Madrid, U.S. news media are still hyping "autonomy" and "limited self-rule" as best for the Palestinian people. But just as counterfeit democracy is a poor substitute for the real thing, stenography for the White House is no substitute for independent journalism.

November 7, 1991

Part XI
Fractured History

Those who look to news accounts for history are condemned to see distortions repeated. What passes into media currency becomes popularized "history" that may have little or nothing to do with what actually took place. Hollywood movies can also distort the past—but don't count on the news establishment to set the record straight.

Bogus History
Muddies Abortion Debate

News media should do a better job of exposing the spurious history that some foes of abortion rights have been using to muddy debate.

Lately they've invoked the name of Martin Luther King Jr. Even conservative commentators, who oppose King's legacy on virtually every issue, claim to be marching with him on abortion.

So do some clerics. New York's Cardinal John O'Connor declared that King would today be an abortion opponent championing "unborn children." Operation Rescue's Rev. Randall Terry has compared himself to the great human rights activist. Terry's followers cite King as they surround abortion clinics and family planning centers with militant "blockades" aimed at intimidating women who might consider entering.

The historical parallels are facile. And false.

The truth is that King never opposed abortion—and there's no evidence he would today.

As early as 1955, he joined Planned Parenthood, endorsing its efforts to provide women access to the widest information about contraception and unwanted pregnancies. In 1966, two years before his death, King co-wrote a speech (delivered by his wife) praising Planned Parenthood founder Margaret Sanger for promoting birth control at a time it was illegal.

And while King sought to secure for blacks their constitutional rights, Operation Rescue has spent years trying to obstruct a woman's constitutional right to choose abortion.

The tactical comparisons are also misleading. King was part of a movement stressing nonviolent tactics that were free of harassment. Yet harassment—of pregnant women and health care workers—has been central to the tactics of Operation Rescue.

Another recent attempt at historical fudging came from the White House. Addressing an anti-abortion rally in January 1992, President Bush called for an end to the constitutional right to abortion by invoking Thomas Jefferson and the Declaration of Independence.

Citing "Jefferson's concept that all are created equal," Bush asserted: "It doesn't say 'born' equal. He says 'created.' From the moment the miracle of life occurs, human beings must cherish that life, must hold it in awe, must preserve, protect and defend it."

To hear Bush tell it, Thomas Jefferson was a genuine anti-choice activist. Most news media offered no contrary information. But history tells a different story.

When Jefferson wrote the Declaration, abortion was legal. And there were few religious sanctions against it either. Throughout the 19th century and into the 20th, abortion was widely practiced in the United States by herbal methods or professional abortionists.

It's interesting to note that in the late 1800s, moves against abortion were led by the American Medical Association (which today supports choice), and were influenced by the Protestant establishment's bigotry against Catholics and fear of falling behind the birth rate of Catholic immigrants.

Even the history of the Roman Catholic Church's position on abortion has been muddied. Catholic teaching has not always held that "abortion is killing." Before 1869, most Catholic theologians taught that the fetus did not become a human being with a soul until at least 40 days after conception, and in some cases later. Abortion before that time was not believed to involve the taking of human life.

Recent NBC News/*Wall Street Journal* polls confirm that most Americans believe "the choice on abortion should be left up to the woman and her doctor." The pro-choice view is even supported by most Republicans (53 percent) and most Catholics (51 percent).

Those who want abortion re-criminalized look to scapegoats to explain how they lost the battle for public opinion. But it can't be blamed on biased news media (both sides have been fully and clearly heard) or on being outspent by the opposition (expenditures have been roughly even).

The majority on abortion is represented by pro-choice advocates. If Martin Luther King were alive, he'd be marching with them.

April 1, 1992

atricia Ireland, president of National Organization for Women (NOW)

The Martin Luther King
You Don't See on TV

It's become a TV ritual each year on Martin Luther King's birthday: the perfunctory network news reports about "the slain civil rights leader."

The remarkable thing about this annual review of King's life is that several years—his last years—are totally missing, as if flushed down a memory hole.

What TV viewers see is a closed loop of familiar file footage: King battling desegregation in Birmingham (1963); reciting his dream of racial harmony at the rally in Washington (1963); marching for voting rights in Selma, Alabama (1965); and finally, lying dead on the motel balcony in Memphis (1968).

An alert viewer might notice that the chronology jumps from 1965 to 1968. King didn't take a sabbatical at the end of his life. In fact, he was speaking and organizing as diligently as ever. Almost all of these speeches were filmed or taped. But they're not shown today on TV.

Why?

It's because national news media have never come to terms with what Martin Luther King Jr. stood for during his final years.

In the early 1960s, when King focused his challenge on legalized racial discrimination in the South, most major media were his allies. Network TV and national publications graphically showed the police dogs and bullwhips and cattle prods used against Southern blacks who sought the right to vote or to eat at a public lunch counter.

But after passage of civil rights laws in the mid-1960s, King began challenging the nation's fundamental priorities. This was the *uppity* Martin Luther King scorned by many media. Today, instead of providing the full story, network television offers us an edited-for-TV character that Jesse

Jackson has dubbed "the harmless dreamer."

The real Martin Luther King spent the last years of his life taking on the Washington establishment. King maintained that civil rights laws were empty without "human rights"—including economic rights. For people too poor to eat at a restaurant or afford a decent home, King said, anti-discrimination laws were hollow. He saw the violent upheavals in the ghettos of the North and West as calls for a national effort to eradicate poverty.

Noting that most Americans below the poverty line were white, King's approach to issues evolved from a racial to a class perspective. He decried the huge income gaps between rich and poor, and called for "radical changes in the structure of our society" to redistribute wealth and power.

"True compassion," King declared, "is more than flinging a coin to a beggar; it comes to see that an edifice which produces beggars needs restructuring."

By 1967, King had also become the country's most prominent opponent of the Vietnam War, and a staunch critic of overall U.S. foreign policy, which he deemed militaristic. In his "Beyond Vietnam" speech delivered at New York's Riverside Church on April 4, 1967—a year to the day before he was murdered—King called the United States "the greatest purveyor of violence in the world today."

From Vietnam to South Africa to Latin America, King said, the U.S. was "on the wrong side of a world revolution." King questioned "our alliance with the landed gentry of Latin America," and asked why the U.S. was suppressing revolutions "of the shirtless and barefoot people" in the Third World, instead of supporting them.

In foreign policy, also, King offered an economic critique, complaining about "capitalists of the West investing huge sums of money in Asia, Africa and South America, only to take the profits out with no concern for the social betterment of the countries."

You haven't heard the "Beyond Vietnam" speech on

network news recently, but national media heard it loud and clear back in 1967—and loudly denounced it. *Time* called it "demagogic slander that sounded like a script for Radio Hanoi." The *Washington Post* patronized that "King has diminished his usefulness to his cause, his country, his people."

Life magazine questioned King's right to dissent "when he connects progress and civil rights here with a proposal that amounts to abject surrender in Vietnam, and suggests that youths become conscientious objectors."

In King's view, the Vietnam War was diverting billions of tax dollars from U.S. cities and the poor: "The war on poverty is being defeated on the battlefields of Vietnam." But his efforts to link the anti-war and civil rights movements rankled the so-called liberal media. The *New York Times* lectured that Vietnam and racism were "distinct and separate" issues; merging the two did a "disservice to both" and led to "deeper confusion."

In his last months, King was organizing the most militant project of his life: The Poor People's Campaign. He crisscrossed the country to assemble "a multiracial army of the poor" that would descend on Washington—engaging in civil disobedience at the Capitol, if need be—until Congress enacted a poor people's bill of rights. *Reader's Digest* warned of an "insurrection."

King's economic bill of rights called for massive government jobs programs to rebuild America's cities. He said that while integrating lunch counters cost the national budget no money, ending poverty would cost billions. King felt militant action was needed to jar a Congress that demonstrated its "hostility to the poor"—appropriating "military funds with alacrity and generosity," but providing "poverty funds with miserliness."

King's efforts on behalf of the poor people's mobilization were cut short by an assassin's bullet. In the quarter-century since then, the federal government has never committed itself to ending poverty.

Remember—since the TV networks won't emphasize it—that 1993 marks the 25th anniversary of the Poor People's Campaign.

Remember, too, that when King embarked upon that campaign, his main foes were not right-wing Republicans or Southern racists—but a White House and Congress controlled by Democrats.

And a media establishment that found King too uppity.

January 13, 1993

Malcolm X and Spike Lee
Versus the News Media

What would Malcolm X say if he could see his name on a thousand theater marquees, hear TV anchors praising him as a hero, and behold his image on national magazine covers and a million T-shirts?

One suspects the black revolutionary would have a sardonic comment, like: "This is America's way of saying 'Thank God he's dead.'"

It's ironic that Malcolm X—who evolved from a petty hoodlum to a great moral leader and inspired thousands of activists in the 1960s—would become a media star. During the last months of his life, well after he'd abandoned the Nation of Islam and its anti-white demonology, Malcolm was quite the media critic.

He condemned biased coverage of Africa, and of crime and police misconduct in the black community here at home. He accused the media of being publicists for so-called "responsible Negro leaders," while portraying him and his allies as irrational, hateful extremists.

Two months before he was assassinated at Harlem's Audubon Ballroom, Malcolm addressed a black audience there about the media's influence: "The press is so powerful in its image-making role, it can make a criminal look like he's the victim and make the victim look like he's the criminal. If you aren't careful, the newspapers will have you hating the people who are being oppressed and loving the people who are doing the oppressing."

In his autobiography (compiled by Alex Haley), Malcolm spoke of how "the press, when it wants to, can twist and slant. If I had said 'Mary had a little lamb,' what probably would have appeared was 'Malcolm X Lampoons Mary.'"

Today's Hollywood hero was a media villain when he

died in 1965. The day after the assassination, an error-filled editorial in the *New York Times* blamed Malcolm for his own death, and called him a "twisted man" with a "ruthless and fanatical belief in violence" whose life was "pitifully wasted" because "he did not seek to fit into society or into the life of his own people."

Days later, thousands of "his own people" viewed Malcolm X's body in one of the largest funerals in Harlem's history. Yet mainstream dailies claimed: "The expected crowds did not show up."

Carl Rowan—then the federal government's chief propagandist as head of the U.S. Information Agency and now a leading media pundit—complained that despite his agency's efforts, newspapers across Africa wrote warmly of Malcolm X. Rowan dismissed him as "an ex-convict, ex-dope dealer who became a racial fanatic."

Yesterday's "ruthless fanatic" has become today's hero with the help of filmmaker Spike Lee, who himself has had a strained relationship with "the white media"— though he's proven to be an adept manipulator of the media.

Besides bringing his powerful "Malcolm X" epic to the screen, he orchestrated massive advance publicity by provoking various skirmishes with the media. To say Spike Lee is a shrewd self-marketer is not to say that his media criticism is wrong.

Lee was denounced as a racist when he stated his preference (reported as a "demand" in some quarters) that media outlets send black journalists to interview him about "Malcolm X." One suspects Lee knew this request would generate exactly the controversy it did—and more free publicity for his film.

He defended his request by arguing that black journalists might bring a keener sensitivity to the story (possibly true); that other movie directors have been allowed to pick and choose the journalists who cover them (definitely true); that media need to be prodded into hiring more black journalists (most definitely true), and finally, that white journalists repeatedly ask questions and file stories that subject Lee to double standards.

Lee said his request for African-American journalists was aimed at exposing that blacks comprise only 4.8 percent of daily newspaper staffs nationwide.

There is historic precedent for Lee's request. In the 1930s, Eleanor Roosevelt's insistence that women cover her news conferences was her way of ensuring that each news outlet in Washington had at least one female reporter.

After a "heavy sell" from Lee's camp and an internal staff debate, *Premiere* magazine did assign an African-American to cover "Malcolm X." That debate also led *Premiere* to hire a black editor and a black staff writer.

Lee's complaints about white journalists are as clear as black and white. Take the headline on *Esquire*'s cover, "Spike Lee Hates Your Cracker Ass." Lee says he's never felt that way—"never have, never will."

He says he gets tired of hearing the kinds of questions—"Do you have any white friends?"…"Are you putting your profits back into the community?" etc.—which are not asked of white filmmakers.

"Are you going to make movies," Lee is asked by white reporters, "that aren't about black people?" He wonders how often Woody Allen gets asked why his movies—usually set in multiracial New York City—never feature black characters.

Lee took a media hit for encouraging students to skip school if necessary to see "Malcolm X"—later toned down to a plea that schools assign students to see it. It's worthwhile to note (few media did) that Lee's school class was forced to see "Gone With the Wind"—with its depiction of jolly house slaves.

Spike Lee's hit film is a breakthrough in spreading the word about Malcolm X. But it is only a movie.

As media critic Malcolm X warned in December 1964: "Never accept images that have been created for you by someone else. It is always better to form the habit of learning how to see things for yourself."

November 25, 1992

The Failed Plot to Kill "JFK"

The plot to kill "JFK" has failed. The Oliver Stone movie is alive and well—a box-office smash, having grossed $24 million in its first two weeks.

Despite an effort by powerful news media to destroy "JFK" in the eyes of the public, Americans are turning out in droves to see a movie the journalistic elite has assailed as paranoid and irresponsible. The anti-"JFK" bombardment began a full seven months before the movie opened.

Now that the American people have foiled the plot— by making up their own minds about the movie—it gives us an opportunity to take a look at the anti-"JFK" plotters: who they are and why they acted.

"Why" is easy to answer. The motive is clear: If national news media did not savage the Stone film as an irresponsible fantasy, then they'd have to explain their own 28-year history of often absurd defenses of the flawed Warren Commission inquiry and its finding that Lee Harvey Oswald acted alone. Indeed, the factual and artistic license taken by Oliver Stone in creating his movie often pales in comparison to the gross inaccuracies peddled in national news reports over the last three decades.

Which brings us to the "who" question. The news outlets who have attacked "JFK" the most vociferously are usually the ones with the longest records of error and obstruction.

Dan Rather

Right before the movie opened, CBS anchor Dan Rather asked of "JFK": "Is it an outright rewrite of history?" The fact is that on the day after the assassination, as the CBS reporter covering JFK's trip to Dallas, Rather rewrote the most important piece of evidence in the case: the Zapruder film.

The first journalist to view the 20-second film of the

assassination taken by Abraham Zapruder with his home movie camera, Rather reported to a national audience that the fatal head shot drove Kennedy "violently forward." As viewers of "JFK" know, the Zapruder footage shows just the opposite: Kennedy's head is driven violently backward, suggesting the fatal shot had been fired from in front of JFK, from the grassy knoll area. But the government theory, announced within hours of the killing, had all shots fired by Oswald from behind JFK in the Book Depository.

Dan Rather has explained his error as one made in a rushed state, after viewing the footage once without benefit of note-taking. Is it possible his ears were so attuned to what the government was saying about the crime that he couldn't see with his own eyes?

In "JFK," the reaction of Kennedy's head to the fatal shot is described as "back and to the left...back and to the left." It wasn't Stone who was wildly wrong on this point. It was Rather, whose rise up the CBS ladder was aided by major reporting assignments on documentaries that did evidentiary somersaults in defense of the Warren Commission.

Time-Life, Inc.

The media conglomerate paid $150,000 to buy all rights to the Zapruder film, and instead of making it available to experts or journalists, spent most of the next decade trying to prevent the footage from being seen or studied. Although Stone has been accused of loading "JFK" with every conspiratorial innuendo, he didn't mention that *Life* publisher C.D. Jackson, who ordered the Zapruder film kept from public view, was a close CIA associate.

While hoarding the Zapruder film, *Life* magazine repeatedly distorted what the footage showed. One *Life* article claimed that the fatal shot caused Kennedy's "skull to explode forward." Another argued that Oswald had shot JFK in the throat from the rear by claiming—falsely—that the film showed the president turning far around to wave to someone in the crowd.

When the Warren Report was issued, *Life* selected Gerald Ford, a commission member, to assess the commission's work. He was uncritical. Meanwhile, *Time* magazine assailed Warren Commission critics as "leftists," "Communists," or, in the case of Bertrand Russell, "that sometime philosopher."

Six months before "JFK" opened, with the movie only half-filmed, a *Time* headline referred to Oliver Stone's "strange, widely disputed take on the Kennedy assassination."

New York Times

The "newspaper of record" has broken all records in heavy lifting for the Warren Commission. From day one in Dallas to opening night for "JFK," the *New York Times* has specialized in the selective usage of evidence while denouncing people like Oliver Stone for doing the same.

Besides publishing editions of the Warren Report, the *New York Times* compiled a book, *The Witnesses*, which purported to offer the highlights of testimony before the commission. The book included a witness's statement that he'd seen a man with a rifle on the sixth floor of the Book Depository, but not his testimony that he'd actually seen two men there and that an FBI agent told him to "forget it." Deleted from the testimony of Abraham Zapruder and many others were their assertions or impressions that shots came from in front of JFK, not from the Book Depository.

Omitted from the testimony of the autopsy surgeon was the bizarre admission that he'd burned the notes and draft of his autopsy. Deleted were the remarks of Oswald's Marine Corps buddy referring to Oswald as a very poor marksman. Researcher Jerry Policoff described the book as "little more than deliberately slanted propaganda."

After the House Assassinations Committee concluded in 1979 that two gunmen had probably fired at JFK, the *Times* remained tenacious in denial of conspiracy: "To the lay public, the word 'conspiracy' is freighted with dark connotations of malevolence perpetrated by enemies. But 'two maniacs instead of one' might be more like it."

Which is more absurd: Oliver Stone's conspiracy theory or the *New York Times'* invention of the "two maniacs" theory? With Oswald dead, presumably it was the other "maniac" who orchestrated the massive cover-up of evidence inside the Federal bureaucracy. Ironically, the *Times'* critique of "JFK" was headlined: "Does 'JFK' Conspire Against Reason?"

Washington Post

Throughout the 1960s, the *Washington Post* denounced proponents of a JFK murder conspiracy as irresponsible kooks. But in 1976, the *Post* promoted its own kooky conspiracy theories…as long as the finger pointed at Fidel Castro. One *Post* article speculated that Kennedy was killed by a conspiracy of Castro and the Mafia (who'd been thrown out of Havana by Castro). Seven months before "JFK" opened, the *Post* returned from kookdom to denunciation mode, accusing Stone of exploiting "the edge of paranoia."

If Stone is "paranoid" to believe that CIA and military rightists were involved in the JFK assassination and cover-up, what of the elite media's slavish acceptance of even more far-fetched theories? That the grassy knoll witnesses were all deluded; that one bullet caused seven wounds in Kennedy and Governor John Connally, shattering major bones, and emerged nearly pristine; that Jack Ruby was no more than a "patriotic nightclub owner"; that Oswald had no links to U.S. intelligence agencies in getting to or from the Soviet Union.

Oliver Stone made a Hollywood movie and chose a flawed hero in District Attorney Jim Garrison to drive his drama (along with some debatable assumptions about Kennedy's plans to change U.S. policies). Stone says he opted not for literal truth but for a "higher truth" and offered his "myth" to counter the "lone assassin myth." Stone, after all, served up a fictional/dramatic work, albeit heavily laden with history and politics.

What excuse do national news outlets have? Journalists aren't supposed to deal in myth but in facts. They utterly failed in the JFK murder case. Perhaps that explains the viciousness of their attacks on "JFK."

January 15, 1992

Part XII
And So It Goes

Calculation and incompetence, insight and propaganda, the vacuous and the venal...these are all ingredients in the mix of news industry products. Alert media consumers may wonder whether to laugh or cry, or scream. Whatever our responses, they should include an active challenge to the media status quo.

P.U.-litzer Prizes for Foulest Media Performances

Every profession likes to honor special merit within its field by handing out annual awards. That's especially true for journalists, who have the bonus of guaranteed publicity—apt to be particularly lavish on the airwaves or in the pages of the winning media outlet.

The following awards do not recognize winners so much as losers—the media consumers. We call these awards "P.U.-litzers," highlighting some of the sorriest and smelliest media performances of 1992. Don't expect the "winning" outlets to crow about these awards.

Best Journalist in a Supporting Role—ABC's ANN COMPTON.

Near the end of the '92 campaign, President Bush appeared at a Waffle House restaurant to convey that Bill Clinton "waffles" on the issues. When Bush's speech neglected to mention waffling, a big-league TV correspondent had this reaction, according to the *Washington Post*: "Ann Compton of ABC News moves urgently from one [Bush] staffer to another…. She tells each one: If you want Waffle House, we need Bush to say something about waffling!" In TV news lingo, Compton wanted a soundbite to go with her photo-op.

Bush finally alluded to Clinton's waffling, but Compton was unsatisfied. "It's still not quite right," she complained to the Bush campaign's press secretary. Here was a reporter helping the president package an attack on his opponent.

TOM TOMORROW ©91

Prize for Ability to Divine Immigration Status—KABC-TV IN LOS ANGELES.

During the L.A. riots, while live cameras showed some Latinos looting a store, a KABC-TV anchor asked his on-the-street reporter if they looked like "illegal aliens." The reporter replied, "Yes."

Dubious Sources—*NEW YORK TIMES,* CNN (TIE).

An April 20 *New York Times* news article on domestic violence against men prominently featured George Gilliland Sr., a "men's rights" advocate who argued that the system is biased in favor of abusive women. The article failed to mention that this source had a violent history, and that several of his ex-wives sought court protection from him.

On Jan. 31, CNN featured perennial foreign policy expert Henry Kissinger, arguing that the U.S. was overly concerned about human rights in China. CNN viewers were not told that the Kissinger & Associates consulting firm specializes in "opening doors" for companies planning to invest in China. Nor that Kissinger headed China Ventures, a company aimed at launching joint ventures with China's state bank.

Leave Education to Beaver Award—TOO MANY WINNERS TO NAME.

When the 1990 Children's Television Act passed, TV stations across the country rushed to comply with the law's requirement for educational programming...by explaining how their existing shows (such as "Leave It to Beaver," "The Flintstones," "G.I. Joe") were in fact educational.

One station cited a cartoon in which "good-doer Bucky fights off the evil toads," explaining that "issues of social consciousness and responsibility are central themes of the program." Another station cited the educational value of "Santa Claus Is Coming To Town," which "answers some of the mysteries, myths and questions surrounding the legend of Santa Claus."

[In March 1993, the Federal Communications Commission finally indicated it would not accept the claims of TV broadcasters that cartoons featuring the likes of Fred and Wilma fit the "educational" bill.]

Quickest TV About-Face Since Gomer Pyle—RUSH LIMBAUGH.

From his Sept. 14 premiere until Election Day, Rush Limbaugh used his syndicated TV show—in some of the most partisan broadcasts in television history—for 22-minute monologues in support of President Bush's reelection. He regularly questioned the intelligence of anyone planning to vote for Clinton—whose policies, Limbaugh said, would wreck the country. No sooner did Clinton win the election than Limbaugh reversed course, telling his TV audience to cheer up: Clinton, after all, had won because he enunciated solid conservative principles.

Best Commentary with Class—ROBERT NOVAK, MONA CHAREN AND *NEW YORK TIMES* (TIE).

In the midst of a Democratic campaign that received more corporate backing than any in party history, the Democrats published a platform extolling free enterprise: "We honor business as a noble endeavor." The platform was instantly critiqued on CNN as "anti-capitalist" by Robert Novak and as "mildly socialist" by Mona Charen.

Ever wary of uncharted waters, the *New York Times* editorialized (June 3) that the Perot campaign "may portend a scary future, leading away from the certitudes of two-party politics to a system open to manipulation by the super-rich." Thank God for today's certitudes: two-party politics full of manipulation by the super-rich.

Comeback of the Year...NOT!—FINANCIAL ANALYST GRAEF CRYSTAL.

For years, Graef Crystal was the expert who estimated the income levels of corporate execs for *Fortune* magazine. In 1991 he was pressured out of his job after calculating that the head of Time Warner, which owns *Fortune*, had earned $78 million the previous year in salary and stock options. Crystal made a comeback with *Financial World* magazine. But he was fired this February after advertisers complained about Crystal's reporting on the exorbitant pay of their chief executives.

"You'll Never Review in This Town Again"—*VARIETY* AND *WASHINGTONIAN* (TIE).

Writing in *Daily Variety*, movie critic Joseph McBride attacked Paramount Pictures' $42 million political thriller, "Patriot Games," as "an expensive stiff" that was "mindless, morally repugnant and ineptly directed." Days later, Paramount pulled its advertising from the publication. *Variety* editorial director Peter Bart also took action: He apologized in a letter to the studio, rewrote the offending review, and promised that McBride "will not review any more Paramount films."

Movie critic Pat Dowell quit her post at the *Washingtonian* after the magazine's editor spiked her positive mini-review of Oliver Stone's "JFK"—which linked official Washington to an assassination cover-up. Editor Jack Limpert defended the censorship in a letter to his former reviewer: "My job is to protect the magazine's reputation and it seemed to me that Stone's film went to the heart of what kind of city this is."

Back to the Closet Award—WRITER SALLY QUINN.

After the National Organization for Women's president Patricia Ireland disclosed her bisexuality, Sally Quinn wrote a *Washington Post* column warning that the women's movement would be seen as "a fringe cause, with overtones of lesbianism and man-hating." Quinn elaborated on her column in an interview: "I agree with everything that gay rights supporters think. I'm just saying you should keep it to yourself if you're a lesbian."

See-No-Holocaust Journalism—*BUSINESS WEEK.*

A Sept. 7 short in *Business Week* sought to explain why proposals by the National Commission on AIDS had not been adopted. Only one source was quoted, Albert Jonsen of the University of Washington: "The impact of AIDS is not great enough to mobilize the kinds of energies that those recommendations require." Because AIDS has mainly affected gays and "marginalized, ghettoized communities," said *Business Week*'s sole source, "the social impact has not been very great."

Well, these are the winners of this year's P.U.-litzers. The competition was fierce.

December 23, 1992

Rush Limbaugh in Bush family box at '92 Republican Convention

Bill Clinton,
Meet the *Washington Times*

From the outset, the news media should subject Bill Clinton's presidency to tough scrutiny. He deserves no deference—only fairness and accuracy.

But President Clinton is likely to get neither from a new neighbor with inordinate clout—the *Washington Times*—a daily like no other in the country.

The *Washington Times* is owned by the Rev. Sun Myung Moon's Unification Church, which subsidizes the paper at a loss of about $35 million per year to attack politicians who don't follow its right-wing agenda.

That attack comes not just on the editorial pages, but—more importantly—on the front page as well.

While an adversarial relationship between press and politicians is essential, the *Washington Times* ignores basic rules of fair-minded journalism when it comes to pillorying the politicians it dislikes. And when the *Times* breaks a "story," it often becomes "news" in other mass media.

Take the story of Bill Clinton's one-week Moscow trip during the first days of 1970.

In a last-ditch effort to derail the Clinton presidential campaign, the *Washington Times* converted innuendo, half-truths and 1950s-style Red-hunting into a crusade about Bill Clinton's "unusual trip" to Moscow where he may have been "duped by Soviet intelligence officials."

After the *Washington Times* front-paged the story, it was pushed by Rush Limbaugh and other media—and ultimately by George Bush, who demanded that candidate Clinton "level with the American people."

The page-one article of Oct. 5, 1992, headlined "Clinton Toured Moscow at War's Peak" (which ran with a companion piece, "Clinton Visit Fit Kremlin's Tailored-for-Tourists Model"), was vintage *Washington*

Times. It was loaded with Cold War sources who refused to be identified—even though the Cold War is over.

Imparting a subversive spin to the Clinton trip were "a British Soviet specialist who advises defense and intelligence agencies," "a top official in Britain's MI5 intelligence at the time," and "a former Soviet official who took part in efforts to influence Western public opinion."

Despite the impressive-sounding descriptions, none of the unnamed experts seemed aware of one essential fact: Clinton's trip to Russia was so *usual* that 50,000 Americans were visiting the Soviet Union yearly at the time, including about one-fourth of the Rhodes Scholars in Bill Clinton's class at Oxford.

It's not surprising that George Bush picked up the *Times'* smear. The paper has enjoyed a special relationship with the White House since its launch a decade ago, receiving leaks and inside information that other papers have not. President Reagan swore by the *Washington Times*; Bush had intimate lunches with the paper's editors.

According to a January 1992 *New York Times* report, it is this power to influence and proselytize that explains why Rev. Moon has happily sustained the small daily, in spite of a cumulative loss estimated at $400 million over 10 years. Though its circulation is believed to be only 100,000 (actual numbers aren't audited), it reaches powerful D.C.-based politicians and journalists.

Many mainstream media unskeptically pick up *Washington Times* stories despite the paper's history of fact-twisting—and despite the resignations in 1984 and 1987 of top editors who charged Unification Church officers with meddling in the paper's editorial process.

The *Washington Times'* forte is to elevate innuendo into news, always against well-targeted liberal or centrist politicians. In August 1988 the paper helped turn a false rumor, that Democratic candidate Michael Dukakis had a history of psychological depression, into front page news: "Dukakis Psychiatric Rumor Denied," read the headline. President

Reagan then made the fable big news across the country when he jokingly called Dukakis "an invalid."

You've heard of the "insanity defense." The *Washington Times* employs the "insanity offense"—imputing mental problems to disfavored politicians. Upset with Republican David Durenberger, chair of the Senate Intelligence Committee at the time, the newspaper unleashed a two-part front page "exposé" in 1986, diagnosing the senator as having "mental health traumas" that could pose a national security risk.

Part of the evidence of Durenberger's "instability" was his "meddling" in foreign policy—criticizing such *Times*-endorsed enterprises as Star Wars and the Nicaraguan Contra guerrillas. (Meanwhile, the *Times* used its front page to solicit funds for the Contras.)

The day before a major 1987 peace march in Washington opposing Contra aid, the *Washington Times* served up an evidence-free lead story on page one that could have been written by Joe McCarthy: "Sandinistas, Qaddafi Fund U.S. Protest." When we confronted a leading *Times* columnist about the smear, he argued that the onus was on us to disprove the wild charge, not on his paper to prove it.

In 1993, for the first time in its life, the *Washington Times* will have a target—instead of a friend—in the Oval Office. Expect the smears to come fast and furious.

And watch to see if the rest of the mass media allow a disreputable paper to push rumor and innuendo into the news.

November 4, 1992

National Public Radio: Serving the Public?

For millions of people, National Public Radio is a daily oasis in the midst of a vast broadcasting wasteland.

Around the country, many NPR listeners consider "Morning Edition" and "All Things Considered" to be in-depth news programs unmatched on the radio dial.

NPR's reputation has grown steadily since 1971, when the fledgling network pledged to supply the nation with independent radio journalism rather than furthering "corporate gain." But how well is NPR fulfilling its pledge in the 1990s?

To answer that question, sociologist Charlotte Ryan (affiliated with Boston College) examined the transcripts of every weekday broadcast of NPR's two news shows—totaling 2,296 stories—during the last four months of 1991. The findings may tarnish NPR's image as a reliable alternative to standard media.

Yes, the noncommercial radio network often produces poignant human-interest features. But NPR's routine reporting and analysis of news events usually remain in sync with official viewpoints. In fact, the study described NPR's dominant news slant as "Beltway Bias"—defined as "the tendency to allow Washington officials and establishment pundits to set the news agenda."

● **Sources:** In selecting and quoting sources, NPR relies most heavily on government officials (26 percent of all sources). Journalists, academics, lawyers and all other professionals combined account for another 37 percent. The gender gap among NPR's sources—including both "newsmakers" and news analysts— is severe: 79 percent are men.

● **Think Tanks:** In Washington—where 28 percent of NPR's domestic stories originate—there are think tanks of every sort. But NPR turned repeatedly for analysis to corporate-funded institutions of the establishment center (such as Brookings, 11 quotes) and the right (such as American Enterprise, 8 quotes). Think tanks that are left-of-center or allied with labor were generally ignored: for example, the Institute for Policy Studies was never quoted.

● **Public Interest Experts:** A long-standing critique of "Nightline," "The MacNeil/Lehrer NewsHour" and other TV news programs has focused on the virtual exclusion of representatives from public interest and citizen action groups. Such experts were no more audible on NPR—only 7 percent of total sources. The number of advocates for any single movement was tiny—racial or ethnic groups (1.5 percent); organized labor (0.6 percent); feminism (0.4 percent); environmentalism (0.3 percent); gay rights (0.2 percent).

● **Regular Commentators:** NPR news executives will argue that they are not to blame for heavily quoting newsmakers such as government officials—who are overwhelmingly white males. But NPR alone *is* to blame for its failure to choose a cast of commentators who "look like America." Of 27 commentators who appeared twice or more during the four months, 26 were white. Only four were women. In other words, 85 percent of them were white men.

"While NPR's special series and cultural reporting reflected considerable diversity," the study concludes, "its day-to-day coverage of politics, economics and social issues, as well as its regular commentaries, did not come close to reflecting the ethnic, gender or class composition of the American public."

The study, commissioned by FAIR (with which we are associated), faulted NPR for generally adhering to news habits found in the rest of the national media—"equating the working of public officials with news" and "equating balance with interviews with the top-ranking member of each major party."

The point is not that NPR should ignore what the President and Congressional leaders say or do, but that it should draw on wide-ranging sources to assess such events. Confining on-air discourse to the spectrum of opinion in vogue along Pennsylvania Avenue does not begin to present the debates going on throughout society.

In-depth newscasts can puncture the doubletalk that often surrounds official pronouncements from Washington or Wall Street—but only by airing the views of diverse, independent analysts and commentators. That's also the way to put the public in public radio.

When hundreds of NPR-affiliated stations beseech listeners to send in donations during pledge drives, "Morning Edition" and "All Things Considered" are praised as alternative sources of news. But when NPR reporters go about their jobs of covering national affairs, they seem to operate as players in Washington's corridors of power—functioning like, and ultimately sounding like, their colleagues in corporate-owned media.

NPR's shift from a fresh, independent news upstart to a more establishment outlet has been so gradual since the 1970s that many listeners have been in a position akin to the proverbial frog: immersed in a pot of slowly heated water, failing to notice as it approaches boiling.

In the arid terrain of American radio, listeners still have reason to tune into NPR news programming. But too often, what we hear are lengthier versions of commercial media outlooks—more committed to official sources and conventional wisdom than independent news and democratic discourse.

March 24, 1993

Wanted:
Full-Disclosure Book Reviews

Imagine you've finished writing a book after several years of research that involved more than 500 interviews, thousands of documents and travels halfway around the world.

The final manuscript is lauded by prominent journalists Seymour Hersh, Stanley Karnow and Mike Wallace. The History Book Club signs on. And the key trade magazines of the book business give an emphatic thumbs-up. Even *Kirkus Reviews*, known for its stinginess with accolades, praises your 559-page book as "brilliantly reported."

But then you find out that the country's most powerful judge of new books—the *New York Times Book Review*—assigned yours to a reviewer who works for an institution that you've criticized in the book!

This is exactly what happened to journalist David E. Kaplan, whose book *Fires of the Dragon* was published in October 1992. Subtitled *Politics, Murder, and the Kuomintang*, the book documents four decades of covert manipulation inside the United States by Taiwan—the island nation that Washington long pretended was "China."

Kaplan shows how agents of Taiwan went beyond spying and disinformation. In 1984 they murdered an American citizen in his home near San Francisco. The victim, Henry Liu, was a journalist and espionage figure who had written a critical biography of the head of Taiwan's ruling Kuomintang party, Chiang Kai-shek's son Chiang Ching-kuo.

One of the most effective weapons in Taiwan's public-relations arsenal has been money—lots of it—bankrolling American scholars, and influential think tanks in Washington.

"The American Enterprise Institute admitted receiving between $300,000 and $400,000 a year from Taiwan sources," Kaplan reported near the conclusion of his book. AEI, a conservative think tank, is a major player in Washington.

Since Kaplan's book specifically criticizes the American Enterprise Institute for its lucrative connection with Taiwan, why publish a review by Nicholas Eberstadt— someone who has been working for AEI since 1985?

"It was our decision that that was not a sufficient conflict of interest for us to pull the book back from him," according to Barry Gewen, the *New York Times* staffer who handled the review.

"I just know that Eberstadt is a decent, honorable fellow," said Rebecca Sinkler, editor of the *New York Times Book Review*. The book's brief criticism of Eberstadt's employer "is one of those gray areas," she told us. "To some degree, at one point or another, you have to trust people. And I trust Nicholas Eberstadt."

Eberstadt was candid with his editors—though, as it turned out, not with his readers—about the conflict of interest.

"I checked twice with the editors at the *New York Times Book Review*, once when the book was suggested and I mentioned to them that AEI received money and funding from Taiwan, secondly when I informed them that there was specific mention and criticism of American Enterprise Institute," Eberstadt told us. "Both times I checked to see whether they felt that I should continue reviewing the book, and both times they said yes indeed."

In the end, AEI's Eberstadt did not like *Fires of the Dragon* very much. His review, published Oct. 25, 1992, gave credit for "vivid" crime reportage but deemed the book substantially flawed—declaring it "poor history."

Eberstadt, whose think tank has received big money from Kuomintang-run Taiwan, concluded that "the author's unbridled outrage against the Kuomintang detracts not only from his historical analysis, but even from his detective story."

Nowhere did Eberstadt's review mention the book's key theme: Taiwan's multifaceted intervention in the internal affairs of the United States.

Emphasizing the pernicious effects of Taiwan's funding of American academics, Kaplan's book explains that publications by these scholars have failed to mention the Taiwanese money: "Had the authors included a disclaimer with their works—that their research was in fact sponsored by agents of a foreign government—one could perhaps judge their scholarship more appropriately."

Ironically, the *New York Times* was guilty of this same breach of ethics when it opted not to inform the review's readers about the reviewer's conflict of interest. For the *Times* to have mentioned it, editor Sinkler told us, "would have thrown it out of proportion."

Yet such an acknowledgement was needed, says Steve Weinberg, who has written on book review ethics for *Columbia Journalism Review*. "There should have been a sentence, or maybe even a paragraph, about David Kaplan's reference to AEI in the book."

In Weinberg's words, "Disclosure is usually the best disinfectant." In its absence, a book review can leave a bad odor.

What happened to *Fires of the Dragon* at the *New York Times Book Review* is certainly not the worst example of improper book-review assignments and undisclosed conflicts of interest. But that's small consolation for David Kaplan, who was dealt a bad hand by a powerful book-reviewing institution that didn't quite manage to deal from the top of the deck.

December 9, 1992

Quayle's Memoirs:
Book Industry Prepares
Another Gem

After Richard Nixon left the White House in disgrace, the Warner Communications media conglomerate paid him $2 million for his memoirs. Certain Warner executives had long been close to Nixon: In 1972, they contributed to his Committee to Re-Elect the President (CREEP), which initiated the Watergate fiasco.

Nixon's book lost a fortune for the publisher.

Now HarperCollins—owned by media mogul Rupert Murdoch—has agreed to pay a reported $1 million for the memoirs of another departing political figure: Dan Quayle.

HarperCollins will be marketing the Quayle book not only through its commercial division, but also to "Christian booksellers" via its religious publishing subsidiary.

Since this is Quayle's first book, we'd like to offer him some advice:

Keep the book short.

As you once said: "Verbosity leads to unclear, inarticulate things." No one knows better than you how much trouble verbosity can cause. Like that time you arrived in American Samoa, and your remarks to the welcoming party went on and on: "You look like happy campers to me. Happy campers you are, happy campers you have been and, as far as I'm concerned, happy campers you will always be."

Quit denouncing the "sophisticates."

During the brouhaha over Murphy Brown, you blasted the cultural elite as a bunch of sophisticates. Stop that. You're an author now. In a country where the average person reads about one book per year, you need all the readers you can find. And that best-selling book by your pal Rush Limbaugh exhausted the quota for most non-sophisticates.

Write for a multicultural audience.

From a marketing perspective, it makes no sense to limit your readership to just white males, or Christian fundamentalists. Enroll in an ethnic sensitivity class. Your book must improve on your original response to the question of whether you have any black friends or staff members you regularly consult with: "Well, Carolyn Washington runs the house, and we see her every day."

Stress your achievements.

Expound on your claim that you are qualified to be president because you know foreign leaders "by their first names." Remind the American public that you're the guy who proposed legislation to give golf pros a special tax break.

Put some mysteries to rest.

For a long time, you said that your favorite movie was "The Candidate" starring Robert Redford—and that it even encouraged you to become a politician. Have you figured out that the movie was not a favorable portrait of American politics?

Dismiss all your bloopers by focusing on that vicious misquote about your Latin America trip.

When you returned from Latin America, you were quoted as saying: "My only regret is that I didn't study Latin harder in school so I could converse with those people." You never said that, but much of the world believes you did. Harp on that quote for a whole chapter. Say it's a typical misquote.

Don't even mention your appearance at the United Negro College Fund luncheon, where you transformed its slogan "A mind is a terrible thing to waste" into "What a waste it is to lose one's mind." Or your comment to Sam

Donaldson on the subject of bloopers: "I stand by all the misstatements that I've made."

Wax so indignant over the Latin misquote that readers might assume those other bloopers were made up, too. Readers may not know the other ones are all on tape.

Fill up half your book with long quotes from the 1992 Washington Post *series that actually took you seriously.*

The *Post* series by Bob Woodward and David Broder—later published as the book *The Man Who Would Be President*—proved that heavyweight journalists can be almost as superficial as a lightweight politician.

Remember how you reacted to the *Post* articles: "No serious journalist can ever again write the Jay Leno caricature," you said. Later that day, you declared that President Bush would "lead us out of the recovery."

Choose a snappy title.

Consider "My Mind Is a Terrible Thing To Waste." Or, "You Can Be a Happy Camper, Too." Or, "The Golf War."

Despite all this sound advice, cynics will complain: Dan Quayle hasn't even read a book, how's he going to write one?

The cynics are wrong. During the 1988 campaign, when asked about "works of literature" that had influenced him, Quayle mentioned a recent work by literary master Richard Nixon. Wife Marilyn Quayle gave a better answer, explaining that her husband "really is the studious sort" who "tries to read Plato's *Republic* every year."

So hail to the authors' club: Plato, Nixon, and now Quayle.

February 17, 1993

Bird-Brained Politicians
Play God

Many politicians insist that the spotted owl should not interfere with cutting down old-growth timber. Sometimes the beleaguered bird—an endangered species—seems to have replaced the Russian bear as the most reviled critter on the planet.

We're told that it's a matter of putting humans ahead of the more lowly of God's creatures. News reports often focus on loggers as the group that is "threatened" or "endangered." One paper's headline read: "Spooked By An Owl, Town Fights For Its Future."

The bird's image has gotten so bad that the front page of a large California newspaper matter-of-factly referred to "the notorious spotted owl." To conservative pundits, the hapless bird has become *the* symbol of "environmental extremism."

When President Bush visited the Pacific Northwest in mid-September 1992, he declared that "it is time to make people more important than owls." A few weeks earlier, Dan Quayle had assured voters in California's Central Valley: "When it comes to talk about priorities between the spotted owl and jobs, we're going to come down on the side of jobs."

But Quayle said something else during that campaign swing—something the national media missed: "Obviously, when you take the bald eagle and things of that sort, of course you're going to make sure that they are saved."

"Obviously"? "Things of that sort"? "Of course"?

Puzzled, we called the vice president's press office for clarification. But none was available. Leaving us to ponder: Why is it so important to sacrifice the spotted owl but save the bald eagle?

And then it became obvious: To Dan Quayle, the bald

eagle is *politically correct.* The spotted owl is not.

After all, you don't see spotted owls on those big U.S. Postal Service full-color Express Mail envelopes. You don't see them on U.S. Savings Bonds, or on coins, or in campaign commercials.

You do see the bald eagle, fierce and graceful. Plenty of sharp claws. Just like politically correct American birds should be. The opposite of wimpy owls that stay in ancient woods, can't stand the light of day, and probably don't give a hoot about advancing the national interest.

At the Republican Convention, Pat Robertson stated it clearly in his speech—the one where he said, "The people of Eastern Europe got rid of their left wingers, it is time we in America got rid of our left wingers!" (If only he could find a bird with two right wings.) The Reverend exclaimed that the Democrats are "running on a platform that calls for saving the spotted owl, but never once mentions the name of God."

In sharp contrast, the Republicans are running on a platform that reveres the bald eagle, and mentions God a lot. You can tell a bird by the rhetorical company it keeps.

Yet surely Vice President Quayle's patriotic ark can hold more than a couple of heavily-hormoned bald eagles in its ornithology berth. The gangplank for Danny's ark should be kept in place for robins, which could be seen as symbolizing the family. Cardinals are dramatic, their name consonant with religious values and their color no longer suspect, so they should be saved too.

But how about, say, the quail? Dan Quayle may quail at the question, but: Would Quayle want to save the quail? Probably not. Just another effeminate bird that can barely fly. You've seen one you've seen them all.

You may think this selection process is for the birds. But if your values are what they should be—American, family, moral, traditional and Western—you'll agree that not all lifestyles are equal.

So from now on, each bird must carry its weight in this

country. No more freeloading feathered friends. God's word may be final, but even He needs help from patriots.

Dan Quayle has it all figured out: Put Creationism back in the schools, but don't dispense with Darwin entirely. May the birds with the fittest lobbyists survive.

September 23, 1992

Some Advice for Reading Between the Lines

Many people prefer to *read* the news. That's understandable, since print media offer more substance than TV and radio newscasts do. But readers should be alert to hazards of an inky news diet.

News shouldn't be swallowed without healthy doses of skepticism. When reading daily papers and newsweeklies, we need to keep asking ourselves some key questions:

Is the headline out of line?

Often we skim the headlines to catch up on what's happened. But that way we're apt to turn the page with a skewed impression of what the article actually says. Sometimes the gap between headline and story is laughable.

During the Moscow summit in June 1988, headline skimmers may have moved on after seeing "Reagan Impresses Soviet Elite" in big type in the *New York Times*—without reading the text of the article, which indicated that President Reagan had fallen asleep while meeting with Soviet officials.

In another summit article, the *Times* quoted Britain's Margaret Thatcher as saying of Reagan, "Poor dear, there's nothing between his ears." The headline: "Thatcher Salute to the Reagan Years."

Why *those* photos?

Newsweek ended 1992 with a cover story on "Women of the Year," describing female "power players" who are "going to reshape the way Washington does business." But the photographs sent a different message: In four of the nine carefully composed photos, the women were pictured with children (either their own or someone else's). In five of the photos, the women were lying on the floor or otherwise horizontal. It's hard to picture a similar photo spread about male "power players."

The magazine has exhibited a photographic bias for racial stereotypes as well. Although a *Newsweek* cover story about drugs in November 1988 observed that "the Crack Nation includes all sizes, classes and hues," white offenders were absent from the featured photos—which showed black people being arrested, on trial, and en route to prison.

Who are the sources?

Many news stories are built on official sources—often identified only as "senior administration officials," "informed sources," "Western diplomats" and the like. When official sources dominate an article, they tend to determine its slant, especially in the absence of contrary views from policy critics.

Who gets the space every day?

Routine imbalances are taken for granted, even though they're based on no particular logic—only power and precedent.

Virtually every newspaper publishes some kind of "Business" section each day, attuned to the outlooks of corporate executives. But newspapers don't have daily "Labor" pages, focusing on the concerns of working people—who are far more numerous in society than business managers and investors.

Don't assume that Business sections are written for a cross-section of readers. As *Philadelphia Inquirer* reporter David Johnston told us, "The financial pages of the newspapers of this country see the world through the eyes of bankers as opposed to through the eyes of bank customers."

Are euphemisms being deployed?

Sometimes grim historical events receive quite a face-lift in print.

Even colonialism can get plastered with a happy face.

A November 1992 *New York Times* article described the British Empire as having brought "British managerial skills" to India, helping the natives run their plantations. A week later the *Times* reported that British colonial rule in Hong Kong has been a "benign dictatorship."

Human rights abusers can be prettified by journalistic euphemisms. While the U.S.-allied government of Turkey engaged in torture and murder of dissidents during the 1980s, a *Washington Post* news article characterized those activities as "controversial measures." According to the *Post*, Turkey's ruler pursued a "down-to-earth approach" to deal with "the rough and tumble of everyday politics."

Did a bogus lead bury the real story?

In theory the most important facts appear early in a news article. But sometimes a buried tidbit, too little and too late in the article, flies in the face of everything previously reported.

A 50-paragraph article in the *New York Times* in November 1987 hyped the popularity of Nicaragua's Contra guerrillas, and featured a front-page photo of a Contra soldier with an adoring child. Buried near the end of the article was a passing reference to a just-released Americas Watch report stating that "the Contras systematically engage in violent abuses...so prevalent that these may be said to be their principal means of waging war." If so, why weren't Contra abuses—which included the murder of hundreds of children—front and center in the piece?

Are the labels biased?

"Military leader" may not be a negative reference, but "military strongman" certainly is. Panama's Manuel Noriega was always a dictator, but it wasn't until he fell out of favor with Washington in the late 1980s that "military strongman" (or "dictator") became his first name in news dispatches.

In domestic politics, "moderate" is a pleasant-sounding media label to describe politicians unwilling to rock the status-quo boat. But for many people the status quo means suffering that is anything but "moderate."

In coverage of events overseas, U.S. news media are inclined to call a regime "moderate" if it has good relations with the White House. So, Saudi Arabia is "moderate"—which would surprise the torture victims who are inside Saudi prisons due to their political beliefs.

The most difficult biases to detect are the ones that are so common we don't give them a second thought—they simply blend into the familiar media scenery. If we take a fresh look at what passes before our eyes every day, "the news" may never be the same.

March 10, 1993

Index

Index

Civil rights, 18-19, 99-101
Civil Rights Act (1964), 19
Class warfare, 30, 32-35
Clean Air Act, 14
Clift, Eleanor, 23
Clinton, Bill, 8, 10, 198, 220, 223
   and draft dodging, 139-41
   economic plan of, 21, 22, 28-30
   on the environment, 45
   presidential campaign of (1992),
     35, 36-40, 99, 126, 128, 143, 148
   on Sister Souljah, 129-31
   support for gay rights by, 106
   and taxes, 114
   Washington Times coverage of,
     227-30
Clinton, Hillary, 156, 168
"700 Club" (CBN), 154
CNN, 24, 84, 124, 126, 140, 198,
   222. *See also specific programs*
Cobb, Delmarie, 105
Coca-Cola, 9
Cohen, Jeff, 184
Cold War, 227-29
Colson, Charles, 161-62
Columbia Journalism Review, 100,
   119, 236
Committee to Re-Elect the
   President (CREEP), 160, 237
Commoner, Barry, 159
Compton, Ann, 220
Congress, United States, 13, 15,
   38-39, 207-208
Connally, John, 217
Contras,
   Nicaraguan, 154, 161, 195, 230,
     246
Coolidge, Calvin, 3
Corporations, 149
   control over media by, 22, 23,
     90, 91
   media coverage of, 45-47
   political influence of, 13-15
   sponsorship of PBS by, 42-44
   takeover of Democratic Party
     by, 36-40

   see also Tobacco industry; and
     specific corporations
CORU, 194
Cosmopolitan, 51
Couric, Katie, 165-66
CREEP. *See* Committee to
   Re-Elect the President
Cronkite, Walter, 3, 46-47
"Crossfire" (CNN), 127, 140, 171
Crystal, Graef, 224

D

Daily Variety, 224
Dallas Observer, 160
D'Amato, Alfonse, 13
Dan, Dr. Bruce, 57
D'Aubuisson, Roberto, 177
DEA. *See* Drug Enforcement
   Administration
Declaration of Independence, 203
Defense News, 29
Democratic Leadership Council
   (DLC), 38
Democratic National Committee,
   38
Democratic National Convention,
   36-40, 129, 136
Democratic Party, 36-40, 53, 143,
   148, 209
Dershowitz, Alan, 65
"Desert Storm." *See* Gulf War
Disney, Anthea, 51
DLC. *See* Democratic Leadership
   Council
Dole, Bob, 41
Dole, Elizabeth, 124
Domestic violence, 59, 60-65
Donaldson, Sam, 19, 22, 239
"Doonesbury" (Trudeau), 79, 81,
   86
"Do The Right Thing," 99
Dow Chemical, 38, 47
Dowell, Pat, 224
Dow Jones, 6

Index

Credits

Cartoons by Tom Tomorrow: Pages 16, 43, 77, 88, 112, 118, 138, 191, 221, 243.

Cartoons by Matt Wuerker: Pages 25, 55, 83, 102, 115, 144, 157, 163, 170, 176, 196.

Photographs by Jennifer Warburg: Pages 34, 37, 95, 107, 123, 130, 134, 137, 146, 205, 226, 228.

Cartoon on page 12 courtesy of Kirk Anderson, Madison, Wisconsin.

Cartoon on page 39 courtesy of Signe Wilkinson, *Ms. Magazine.*

Photograph on page 66 courtesy of Jim Laurie/*Review Journal.*

Doonesbury Copyright © 1991 G.B. Trudeau. Distributed by UNIVERSAL PRESS SYNDICATE. Reprinted with permission. All rights reserved.

Photographs on page 181 courtesy of Bill Gentile.

About the Authors

Jeff Cohen and Norman Solomon write a syndicated weekly column on media and politics. The column is distributed to daily newspapers by Creators Syndicate, and to weeklies by Alternet. The authors lecture widely on college campuses around the country.

Jeff Cohen is the founder and executive director of FAIR, the media watch organization headquartered in New York City. He has appeared on such programs as CNN's "Larry King Live," "Crossfire," and "Donahue." Cohen has contributed to various books (including *Stenographers to Power: Media and Propaganda)*, and written for publications such as the *Los Angeles Times, Boston Globe, USA Today, Mother Jones* and *Rolling Stone.* He works closely with activist groups across the United States on issues of media bias and censorship. He resides near Woodstock, New York, with his wife and daughter.

Norman Solomon is the author of *The Power of Babble: The Politician's Dictionary of Buzzwords and Doubletalk for Every Occasion,* and coauthor (with Martin A. Lee) of *Unreliable Sources: A Guide to Detecting Bias in News Media.* His news analysis and commentary articles have been published in the *New York Times, Chicago Tribune, Miami Herald, Newsday, International Herald Tribune* and many other newspapers. He has been a guest on C-SPAN, "Crossfire," and NPR's "Talk of the Nation." Solomon is a commentator on politics and media for the Pacifica Radio Network. He lives in the San Francisco area.

The authors can be contacted c/o FAIR, 130 W. 25th St., New York, NY 10001; (212) 633-6700, fax (212) 727-7668. FAIR produces the weekly radio show "Counterspin," and the magazine *EXTRA!* Call 1-800-847-3993 to subscribe to *EXTRA!*

Daily newspapers can arrange for publication of the Cohen/Solomon column by contacting the authors or Creators Syndicate, 5777 W. Century Blvd., Suite 700, Los Angeles, CA 90045; (310) 337-7003.

M

RECT